The Channel's Companion

A Guide for Connecting with the Higher Realms

AMANDA GUGGENHEIMER

Arcadia Press

The Channel's Companion

Published 2012

ISBN 9 780987 162533

For more information: www.amandaguggenheimer.com

Published by Arcadia Press

www.arcadiapress.com.au

Country of publication: Australia

Typeset in Melbourne by Arcadia Press design studio.

The Channel's Companion

A Guide for Connecting with the Higher Realms

AMANDA GUGGENHEIMER

Acknowledgements

Thank you...

To Kay Jones for editing the *Channel's Companion* as meticulously as
you edited our earlier project, *The Light-Worker's Companion*.
~ Thank you Kay for sharing so generously your insights, which
have enriched the book and for your definition of 'The All That Is'.

To James Terry for translating the text into user-friendly
illustrations and for your artwork on the cover.

Contents

Key indicators that this book may be appropriate for you...

Do you have awareness of a spiritual family around you that is calling for connection with you as much as you are reaching out to them?

Do you wish you could reach beyond the physical world and bridge the gap between you and the beings of light you perceive are with you?

Do you long to be a conduit for the higher realms, able to channel messages through to comfort and support other people?

Do you take greater care of your chakras and general energy field, mindful that they are functioning as portals or receptors for this higher information?

Do you feel more attuned to receiving signs from the universe, especially from Nature, and more adept at interpreting the meaning between events that you might once have dismissed as coincidence, but now regard as synchronicity, as if orchestrated by a higher power?

Do you have a yearning to return to earlier beliefs: to recapture faith in and support from the unseen world and the spirits, angels or special beings who you sensed may have accompanied you in the innocence and purity of your childhood?

Do you pray for yourself, the Earth and humanity to awaken and to enter the new era of harmony?

If so, this handbook is designed for you, to reconnect you to the higher realms so that you can feel the joy of connection for yourself, and serve humanity through the strength that connection brings you.

INTRODUCTION

From the Author

It has been almost seven years since *The Light-Worker's Companion* was published. Over this time, the book has reached more people than I ever envisaged and such has been the response that it has now been published in Russian by Sophia Publishing. Intended as a tool to assist spiritual awakening, to accelerate understanding and provide keys for managing Earth assignments, its reception has been both humbling and heartening. In response, I have been encouraged to endeavour to meet the new and emerging aspirations of my readers, especially the call of those who wish to set up a channelling system that will benefit themselves and those around them.

Towards the end of 2011 the final keys required to complete *The Channel's Companion* were awakened in me through dream, meditation and direct channelling. Whilst *The Channel's Companion* might hold immediate appeal for readers who are familiar with *The Light-Worker's Companion*, it is intended equally for those who may be new to some of the terms, yet embrace the fundamental concepts. If the earlier book (which I now see as Book One) laid the base in terms of information, then the present one (or Book Two) builds upon it to offer instructions for connecting with the higher realms and one's spiritual family. With its balanced mix of information and further instruction, and with key concepts reiterated as background for new readers and as revision for others, it can equally stand alone as a guide or work-book for any who aspire to create a bridge and become a channel to the Divine.

Every person has the ability to receive channelled information; that is, with full awareness to establish communication with the higher realms. The focus of the book is to provide a course in opening one's channelling system to one's higher self, to the higher realms, and specifically, to the Spiritual Hierarchy for Earth, the great light structure that houses all humanity. *The Channel's Companion* is presented as a support for those who have been on the path for some time as well as a course for those new to conscious channelling.

In preparing material for *The Channel's Companion*, I have also drawn from my experience of channelling to others in private professional practice, and from my own journey, channelling for myself as a way of understanding events that take place in my life and the lives of those close to me.

Through walking the 'channel's path' I have learnt a great deal about the higher realms and the vast amount of support they offer human beings. I have also learnt that, as a channel or when approaching any channelled information, one must utilize discernment and choose to embrace only what facilitates one's transportation to a higher frequency or level of experience. The information contained therein is offered as a guide, perhaps only as a point of view, and if one finds it is not helpful or beneficial, one should close the book.

The Law of One, which governs the work, also carries with it the notion that what is done, is done for the good of all. For those with whom the information resonates, may this book be a travel companion. As one embarks upon or continues one's journey of awakening to channelling, may the journey be one of enchantment, adventure and inner fulfilment. Regardless of what unfolds in life, with an active channelling system one is always able to enter that gentle place within to ask questions and receive answers. Most importantly, one receives the higher perspective of the situation, providing the insight to transform one's experience of what is happening. One's fears dissolve into wisdom and compassion through working with the higher perspective gained through channelling one's higher self, guides and guardians.

Finally, in releasing *The Channel's Companion* into reader's hands, I wish to express deep gratitude to my readers for encouraging me to share what I have been blessed to receive through channelling, and to the Spiritual Hierarchy for Earth for allowing me to be a caretaker of the keys, offered here in the following pages. As the year 2012 draws to a close, it seems the perfect time for this to occur, and it gives me a great opportunity to invite each of you to step forth and shine your light with me so that together we may raise the vibration of this wondrous planet that is our earthly home.

September 2012

PART ONE

Preparing to Channel

What is Channelling?

In everyday life, a channel is defined generally as a conduit as well as the process of directing energy or mass in a contained way in a specific direction. When a human being becomes a channel for the higher realms, the function of the channel is similar. The human being receives love, universal energy, and information, and guides this transmission into the physical plane using the faculties of his mind and physical body. He becomes a hollow reed to receive and transmit communication from a higher perspective. As a channel, a human being allows his physical body to bridge to the higher realms and become the vehicle that allows the higher realms to interact with the Earth's plane.

Throughout human history, there have been instances of awakened humans fulfilling this role. Now on Earth, more and more human incarnates are volunteering for such a role. Light-workers, people serving the light consciously on Earth, are stepping forward en masse to facilitate interaction between the higher realms and Earth's physical plane.

Every person has the ability to receive channelled information; to establish communication with the higher realms. Nonetheless light-workers training to become channels experience their role in different ways, demonstrating that there is not only one way to channel. Thus a broad definition of channelling is needed to encompass all light-workers and their varying experiences, and to encourage a more open view on the real nature of channelling.

When defining channelling one must consider it not only a transmission of information or energy from the higher realms into the physical plane, but also a communication between an incarnated being and the higher realms. This may be interactive like a conversation between two or more parties and expressed through a range of creative mediums such as painting, drawing, writing, movement, music and dance. Indeed, although the word 'channel' is widely used in spiritual circles and beyond, the technical definition of channelling remains important.

Channelling is defined here as a conscious act, done with full awareness that one is in some form of communication with the higher realms. It remains in essence the accessing of the channelling system in and above the crown chakra, by the human incarnate and the subsequent receiving of information through the channelling system from the Divine or other beings of light in the universe, whether these beings are angels or spirit guides in various forms. If the chakras are understood in specific contexts as energy centres in the human body, the crown chakra on top of the head denotes the aspirational point or higher consciousness: the pinnacle of awareness for seekers world-wide who are striving to connect with the Divine.

The information received in channelling is direct and different from intuition or that which is derived from external aides such as psychic prompts or divination tools. Channelling may, however, be instructional, offering suggestions, soothing, offering gentle and reassuring words, or free of words altogether, presenting as a flow of love and healing energy and a transmission of feeling.

When granted permission from the human incarnate to do so with his or her full conscious intent, the higher realms extend support in the following ways, all of which may be considered channelling:

Transmitting feelings of peace and bliss

Empowering a human with the capacity to perform healing on another person

Bringing practical help to an emergency

Direct communication, either through automatic writing, spoken word or telepathy through the traditional method of transmission (trance-like state) channelling

When choosing to consciously connect to the higher realms and remember how to channel, one gradually becomes aware of the many ways the higher realms bridge to human beings and the vast range of support they provide.

The higher realms may also manifest as physical beings and present messages to a human being through visions and apparitions. Visions sent by the higher realms and received in meditation and dream open doors to the higher realms. It may be considered channelling when information is conveyed through telepathy, defined here as thought transference, where the higher realms send information into one's mind. In some instances, people who have received such visions have reported that the higher being did not communicate telepathically, but simply spoke the words directly as one person would to another. This, therefore, is not considered channelling because the channelling system was not required – i.e. was not needed to be activated - in order to facilitate communication.

Divination tools such as card reading, tea leaves and runes, although not technically channelling (because data has not passed through the channelling system) can serve to help the human incarnate to 'tune in' to channelling and reveal or strengthen the bridge to the higher realms. When animals and birds appear to humans as totems or messengers through oracle or medicine cards, they act as divination tools, creating corridors between human beings and the higher realms. In recent times there has been a wide range of animal totem or medicine cards produced for use as divination tools and also to assist the process of 'tuning in' to one's channelling system. Meanwhile interaction with animals is well documented through books and articles. That there is a great proliferation in such contact these days is not surprising, given the role that trees, animals and nature have always had in bridging awareness, and given the shift in human consciousness occurring now.

Animals and birds may also serve another function, as spirit guides – conduits for the higher realms. Animals and birds may physically present when one is meditating, appear in a vision, or come in a dream and use these opportunities to telepathically communicate with the human incarnate. In these instances when an animal or bird has appeared unexpectedly, one need only allow one's channelling system to open, to receive the message that the creature wishes to share in its role as conduit or messenger for the higher realms.

Indeed, nature will always be the greatest sign giver. Animals, birds, insects and Earth herself remain in direct communication with the angelic realms and enlightened masters. Angelic beings, saints and other spiritual masters can and do instruct nature to bring messages to channels through higher telepathic exchange. Enlightened masters can also step inside birds (shapeshifting) to bring direct communication.

As one works through the five parts of *The Channel's Companion,* one will begin to train oneself to attune to the subtle world, interpreting signs and receiving messages as a channel. This training is a two-fold process of awakening one's own abilities as well as learning how to facilitate healing and transformation in others.

The Channel's Companion is divided into five parts to be used as a course in opening one's channelling system and developing confidence as a professional channel and healer. If using the material as a course, it is preferable to allow a week between each part so that one can properly practise the exercises and integrate the information. The meditation exercises are at the end of each part. It is important to do these meditations after each part to prepare for the part ahead as there is a natural progression from one to the other. Complete the exercises at the end of each part every day for a week before moving on to the next section. This will allow adequate time for the exercises to take effect.

Throughout the text, to maintain the flow of the writing, terminology is generally used in a way that assumes one understands its meaning. For any clarification, please refer to the section at the end, 'Definition of Terms'.

The Call to Channel

The call to channel may come to some spontaneously and quite early, while for others it may appear to be a more gradual process. There are those for whom channelling or awakening to channel is so automatic that the process they encountered prior to becoming a channel was quite short and uneventful in terms of the profound spiritual experiences one might expect.

For some such channels, the process may be so uneventful they question the relevance of their work, their worthiness to do it, whether they are really doing much at all and whether they ever really felt any 'call to channel'. For these ones, training often began many incarnations ago. They may have trained as oracles, seers, shamans, and trance channels of various modalities whether for the purpose of chanting, healing, invoking the holy power for blessings, or entering the body of an animal or bird, to see across the plains of Earth or the passages of time.

These ones enjoy their role because it comes naturally to them. However the same sense of ease does not necessarily extend to all areas of their life and they might struggle in their interaction with humanity and in balancing their role with the expectations of the people they have agreed to serve. Messengers trust the higher realms and finds solace and comfort in their relationship with the spiritual realms they consider home (perhaps a little more so than their earthly domain). They may find solace in solitary pursuits, through meditation, through the dream-state, and in nature where the veils between earthly life and the higher realms are thinner.

These ones are unique for their role is specific. They cannot deviate from their path for very long because every cell in their bodies is programmed to fulfil their task. They were given the mantle of Messenger before they incarnated and asked for all precautions to be taken lest they try to shy away from the responsibility they agreed to take. If and when they try to resign (and they inevitably try at least once due to the difficulty of Earth assignments), their blueprint and body cell memory activate a key that blocks their path and places them in a feeling of stagnation. The key is a protection mechanism that prevents Messengers from deviating from their highest and chosen path. The mechanism leads them to experience the tiresome and frustrating sensation of treading water in their lives. They realise eventually and with some prodding from their higher councils that they cannot truly move forward until they take up their mantle once more and resume their assignment as Messenger.

Some readers may recognise themselves in the above scenario, while some may be new to channelling and the experiences that accompany it. For many the vista may be slowly opening now before their eyes. These ones who are presently awakening to a new level of themselves may have engaged with the concept of channelling and studied its elements in the past, but are now ready to investigate it further. For them, the channelling path develops in this lifetime. Their gentle exploration and integration of spiritual faith and the natural, graceful awakening of the spiritual self nurture their relationship with their channelling system.

Clearing One's Energy Field

The Channel's Companion maintains throughout the text its core message, which is the need to ensure one keeps as a consistent intention the commitment to raising one's vibrational frequency and keep one's energy field clear. Keeping one's energy field clear of debris is important because before opening the channelling system, debris that may cloud the purity of the messages received, must be removed. If one's energy field is polluted, this higher connection is difficult to maintain consistently, with the result that one might receive messages occasionally, but not regularly. The clearer the channelling system, the clearer the messages received. The aim must be to clear and resolve enough debris in order to raise one's vibration above the third and fourth dimensional planes and into the fifth dimension enabling a direct connection with one's higher self and the enlightened masters. A full explanation of the masters and their relationship to channelling can be found in Part Two.

An easy way to clear lower energy quickly is to spend as much time as possible in nature. Whether it is bushwalking, camping, swimming in the ocean or gardening, nature naturally helps transmute this lower debris. Nature helps to clear away environmental electromagnetic pollution and it also has the ability to clear certain levels of astral and etheric debris. Projected thoughts and negative beliefs lessen in their potency when one spends time in nature. Walking in the fresh air clears the mind and the energy field. Etherically, this occurs as the beings of light who live in nature, beings who live in the trees, and the nature spirits work tirelessly to clear away debris in one's energy field. When an initiate rests against a tree and allows the energy of the tree to flow through his body, the tree being – the spirit of life in the tree, works through the energy field very much like a spiritual healer, and transmutes debris effortlessly. Enjoying time in nature is, in many ways, one of the best investments an initiate can make to support his spiritual path and his work as a healer or channel. Nature becomes one's spiritual support and is the ultimate spiritual healer.

The garden cleanses energy fields and helps to anchor human energy into the earthly plane. When one spends time channelling and working with the higher realms, it is important to anchor that energy back into the earth. If one anchors one's energy, one remains levelheaded, sensible and balanced. Sometimes, people on the spiritual path or people working as healers and channels can appear scattered and their energy fields disorderly. When this happens, it can indicate that these individuals have spent considerable time working with energy flowing through them and not enough time anchoring those energies into the physical plane, and specifically into the nature realms.

The act of sending signs through nature can also become a useful tool for the higher realms when their human initiate (the person they serve by being their spirit guide) requires information that he/she is 'missing' or not receiving through the usual way of meditation or channelling. There are various reasons for a channel to 'miss' or overlook information. The information may be disturbing for the person to hear and therefore an unresolved aspect of her is unconsciously blocking it from entering her conscious mind. She may be too busy with the practical tasks of daily life to hear everything she needs to. Her channelling ability may be weak due to tiredness, illness or a natural cycle of rest, which occurs for all channels at various periods in their lives. Through regular interaction with the higher realms the channel learns to attune to signs, recognising that the higher realms use this modality when other methods fail. Through practise, the channel learns to accept the signs in the various forms they arrive, interpret them with accuracy, and integrate the knowledge and wisdom accompanying the sign. More often than not, these signs are from nature and the animal kingdom.

Communing with nature is an essential aspect of taking responsibility for the channel's path. Through connecting with nature, the channel remains anchored into the physical plane and thus very aware of subtle shifts in energy, making the channel more empathetic towards the needs of others and planet Earth. Nature can also act as a guide and guardian. The beings of light of the nature realms communicate through one's channelling system. Tree beings or the spirits of trees, bring messages. While meditating in nature, beings of light in the form of animals or birds may also bring insights, cautioning about something one has not seen clearly, or bringing a fresh perspective if one is uncertain about a particular situation that is unfolding.

The energy field surrounding a human body also responds positively to the healing and cleansing power of water. Swimming in the sea cleanses the energy field of energetic toxins. If the ocean is not accessible, an Energy Field Clearing Bath or Epsom salt bath is an easy alternative with a cleansing effect (see below).

Good indicators that the energy field is polluted and in need of cleansing are:

The information accessed through channelling feels very far away

Answers feel forced

One feels confused or distracted easily while attempting to focus

When one commits first to clearing the energy field of debris, answers will come clearly and immediately. If one's energy field is kept clear consistently, through an ongoing commitment to keeping a vibrant energy field, revitalised with love - even if to do so requires daily cleansing, prayer, affirmation, walks in nature, and meditation, one will be able to receive messages on a consistent basis. A daily practice of cleansing, prayer, affirmation, walks in nature and meditation is well rewarded indeed.

As well as a conscious and ongoing commitment to keeping the channelling system clear, in order to receive information from the higher realms effectively, a channel must deal initially with external debris - pollution or debris in her energy field that does not belong to her and that has accrued over time. Energy fields can be polluted with environmental debris, such as toxins and electromagnetic interference, and debris belonging to others. The debris that belongs to others can store in the energy field over many years, possibly over many lifetimes. This is because at the time of reincarnation, an individual reconnects to his body cell memory and blueprint that he carried throughout all of his past incarnations. This blueprint is an energetic blueprint that each soul carries over lifetimes. All the wisdom he gained over these lifetimes remains in the blueprint as well as anything unresolved. Sometimes thoughts, beliefs about how things should be or what one should do as well

Diagram of a Polluted Energy Field

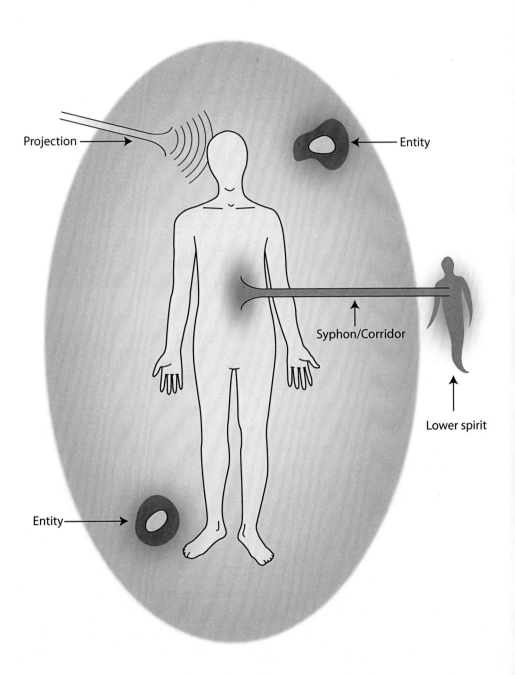

as projections from others, sit in the energy field where they may be readily reactivated. These things may not have originated from the carrier, but may have resulted from interaction with other people and other environments in previous lifetimes.

During childhood, an initiate may adopt unhelpful beliefs belonging to other members of the family or community and these may continue to build up over ensuing years. These belief systems sit in the energy field like a heavy blanket and can cloud the initiate's ability to perceive himself from a higher perspective. These beliefs may cloud his ability to raise his vibrational frequency to the level that allows full connection to the fifth dimension. By clearing this pollution away as it arises, the initiate reaches a level where the energy field becomes relatively self-cleansing so that if a thought, projected by someone else, lodges in the energy field, the change in the energy field is felt immediately. The alien thought is instantly recognisable and immediately transmutable. One may simply surrender it, or bless it and then release it and have it dissolve immediately. The thought will not have the opportunity to settle in the energy field and lower one's vibrational frequency.

External negative thoughts can be a potent force and it is important to understand their workings. In the main, they arise from two main sources. In the first case, they may come from another person or group of people; that is, where an individual, family or community projects thoughts onto a person or group of people that have a negative impact upon that person's or those people's image of themselves. This in turn undermines their feelings of safety and acceptance in the world. An example would be racial prejudice where one group of people in a town forms the view that another group is inferior and/or dangerous. These beliefs, when held strongly enough and projected with sufficient vehemence, have the capacity to penetrate the energy fields of others and plant seeds of self-doubt, which lead to feelings of worthlessness, hopelessness and fear. This can become so entrenched that a third party, even one removed from the initial interaction, might detect the feelings of self-doubt that have been engendered and respond in such a way that the situation is exacerbated.

The second source is the projected thoughts and imprinted belief systems that come from mediums such as television and video/computer games. These devices provide a visual aspect that gives additional power to the

Diagram of a Clear Energy Field

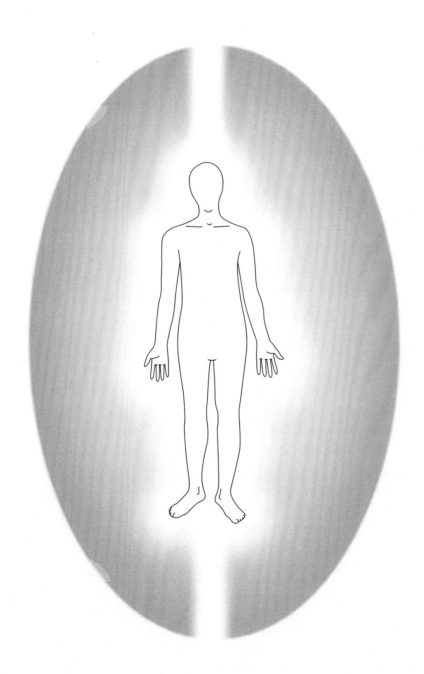

thoughts, enabling them to lodge into the energy field and integrate quickly. Visual images that create insecurity, anger or fear at the first level, may then generate a form of energetic pollution in the energy field. At a deeper level, these visual images may have the capacity to imprint on the body cell memory. This creates an experience in the unconscious mind which may struggle to differentiate between an actual event experienced by oneself, or a witnessed event experienced as an observer. Some initiates may subsequently experience disturbances in their meditations, sleeping patterns and overall sleep quality.

Another form of external debris is environmental pollution, which can come from physical pollution in the air, soil and water, and electromagnetic radiation from electromagnetic frequency generated by electronic equipment. One may want to limit the time spent in energetically unsupportive environments that contain high levels of electromagnetic radiation. Learn to recognise the difference between places that generate positive and invigorating feelings, and those that leave one feeling pessimistic and agitated. Exercise discernment – and elect the former.

Etheric pollution, sometimes called astral plane interference, is yet another form of external debris. This manifests as third dimensional and lower fourth dimensional entities and spirits that have passed over, but have not surrendered the physical plane, and spirits that are attached to people's energy fields. Occasionally, relatives who have passed over and do not feel safe enough to let go of their earthly family to go home to the higher realms, attach to the energy field of a relative. In some instances, spirits who have passed over may not know the person to whom they attach, but may recognise a safe place in the person's energy field where they can reside instead of letting go and passing over fully. These spirits receive doses of energy from the energy field of a live person. This form of astral debris can be a heavy burden to carry and can make it difficult for the human being to reclaim his/her own energetic boundaries. These lower entities can live in a host's energy field for many years, draining energy from the person. The host may feel tired a lot of the time or even aggressive. He may develop personality traits or addictions that belonged to the spirit when it was incarnated in a human body.

It is important to clear these attachments before attempting to channel.

When one channels, one wants to ensure that the messages received are from the fifth dimension and are not the misguided thoughts of a lower entity. A channel must insist on raising her vibrational frequency so that she can connect directly to the fifth dimension and not have any interference on any level from any low frequency in the third or fourth dimension. If one wishes to work professionally as a channel this becomes very important because one does not wish to be in a position where one has accidently channelled a lower vibrational frequency or a lower entity masquerading as a higher entity. One does not want to be responsible for negatively influencing another person because one neglected to clear one's energy field.

Protection from lower entities is a common concern amongst channels. There are two main ways to ensure one is less attractive to lower entities. Firstly, one must clear the debris from the external sources discussed above, out of one's energy field. Secondly, one must heal the unresolved aspects of oneself.

To clear external debris, one can learn to transmute for oneself, which is most useful because to work as a channel one must be clear every day, or enlist the help of a dedicated spiritual healer. Certain monks, nuns, rabbis, priests, medicine men and women, and others aligned to the spiritual path, are trained to clear this debris. They may give this debris a different name, depending on the discipline in which they were trained, but regardless of what name they give it, their commitment to Divine Will ensures the debris is transmuted.

One can also do much to help oneself, and in rather straightforward ways. At its simplest, the energy fields of channels who work with clients require regular cleansing, as does the workroom used to conduct the channelling session. The chanting music of Tibetan Buddhist monks sends a vibration through rooms and clears debris from houses, energy fields, offices and workspaces. Put on a recording of Tibetan chanting throughout the day to cleanse the home or workplace of unwanted energetic debris. The chanting may also be played in the background during a channelling or healing session to harmonise the energy and keep the space clear of debris.

If music is effective in the healing room, it also provides a powerful means for clearing the channel's own energy field, and here personal preference is a key factor, as music to one's liking will almost certainly be the most beneficial. Some may prefer Gregorian chant music, for example, while others might favour instrumental music, such as the gentle sound of the harp. Experiment with the different forms and let the selection be based on what harmonises with one's own signature frequency, for music that simultaneously clears the energy fields of both the room and the practitioner is likely to be doubly uplifting and restorative.

Along with the Energy Field Clearing Bath, cleansing one's energy field through Smudging and the Energy Field Clearing Meditation will significantly reduce the effect of external debris.

Energy Field Clearing Bath

The combination of Epsom salts, crystals and lavender oil work through the layers of the energy field and transmute some of the debris. Lavender, with its blue/violet hue closely linked to the transmutational power of violet light, dissolves debris in the outer layers of the energy field into light and draws upon the violet light of the amethyst crystal to support this transmutational process. Because of its transmutational and cleansing properties, lavender is considered an antiseptic for the energy field. Sea salt and Epson salts have physical cleansing properties, cleaning the skin and the layer of energy closest to the skin.

Tools Needed

1 Cup of Epsom salts

½ Cup of sea salt

Several drops of lavender essential oil

1 small amethyst crystal

1 small clear quartz crystal

1 small rose quartz crystal

Suggested Process

Place all ingredients in the bath and soak in the water for at least 20 minutes to allow enough time for the cleansing to occur.

It is beneficial to do the Energy Field Clearing Meditation outlined on the following page while in the bath.

Smudging

If it is suspected that a lower spirit has attached to your energy field, employ an old method called smudging. Smudging is used by Shamans in smudging ceremonies and by healers to clear astral debris and create a clear space around an individual or group.

Tools needed

A bunch of dried herbs such as garden-variety sage, or if it is available, 'grandfather sage' and dried lavender

Cooking string

Heat resistant bowl or dish

Matches

Suggested Process

Wrap the herbs tightly together with string to create a 'smudge stick'.

Set the tip of the smudge stick alight and then put the flames out, so that the stick smokes like incense. Run the smoke through your energy field in a sweeping motion before using the smoking stick to clear your house or client.

Energy Field Clearing Meditation

Meditation is a proactive way of clearing one's energy field. Practising the following meditation once a day over the next week will assist to develop conscious awareness of what is in one's energy field and help in monitoring the energy field to ensure it remains clear.

Sit or lie down and relax.

Close your eyes and take a deep breath and exhale slowly.

In your mind's eye, visualise stepping beyond your body and peering down over it.

Visualise a bright light like a flood-light shining down on your body from above, lighting up the physical body and the space around the body. The light will highlight the physical body and it will make the energy field transparent. Use this light to study the energy field.

Are there any areas that are not shining brightly under this light? Are there any grey patches? Are there any dark patches? Are there any unfamiliar beings in the energy field?

Shine the spotlight on the energy field. If an area of the energy field seems murky or discoloured, intensify the light, directing it specifically into that area. Allow this bright white light to transmute this murkiness or discoloration. Keep intensifying this light into any areas that seemed discoloured or dark or heavy until those patches are restored to the brilliance of the white light.

Now shine this white light throughout the physical body. Shine it over your head. Are there any strange beings, any pollution or lower vibrational frequencies? Are there lower or foreign thoughts, fears or debris contributing to the grey patch? Shine this brilliant white light around the head until the energy runs clear.

Use the spotlight to trace the boundary of the energy field. The boundary may be several metres beyond your physical body. The light will search for any weakness in this boundary. A strong boundary will appear like a firm film of energy. For rips, tears or patches where there is no boundary at all, use the spotlight to strengthen or rebuild it.

Visualise that you are contained in a shell of energy, the shell acting as a boundary. Stand outside this shell of energy and shine the light to check the boundary. Aim for a very strong outer shell around your energy field so that it can adequately provide shelter from external thoughts and projections that are not your own and do not serve your highest good and will. Repair any weaknesses by flooding the area with light.

Now concentrate the light into the trunk of the body and move the light through it, shining light intensely into your stomach area to dissolve any fear, nervousness, stagnant or unhelpful emotion. Sometimes people and lower spirits siphon energy through the emotional bodies of others by locating weaknesses in the stomach area and solar plexus which house part of the emotional body. It is important to shine light into this area and search for tentacles or cords used by other people or lower entities to inappropriately take energy. These cords do not benefit the person being stolen from or the person or being stealing the energy. While an incarnated person or a being in the spirit world takes energy from another, this will continue until the entity stops taking from others and chooses to return to Divine Source, where an endless abundance of energy is freely available. It is for the benefit of all concerned that this process is expedited. By allowing the light to shine on these cords and dissolve them, you free the person or being from dependency on another being and promote the return of that entity to Divine Source. When a tentacle is removed or a cord cut, the light will follow the cord to the edge of your energy field and seal the corridor.

Most importantly with this type of clearing meditation, allow no area to remain hidden from your inspection. Shine light through every part of the energy field and every area of the physical body. If a particular area is difficult to clear, simply turn up the light, intensify it and keep intensifying it. Eventually it will run clear.

Take a deep breath and return from meditation. If you located any area that resisted turning into clear light, write the details down in a notebook as a reminder to return to it and work on it during the week. Aim to clear the energy field either through meditation, Epsom salt

and crystal baths, asking for nature's assistance, or using the sage stick
by the end of the week.

With ongoing commitment to the process and procedures above, through keeping
the energy field clear, any difficulties one experiences in awakening the channelling
system will lessen in their intensity and efforts to be of service will be rewarded in the
proper time.

PART TWO

Connecting to the Channelling System

Channelling and the Role of the Dimensions

The Channel's Companion introduces the reader to an advanced facility, available to all who wish to communicate directly and clearly with the higher realms. This progressive mechanism is called a channelling system, whose home is in the upper fourth dimension and fifth dimension. The channelling system provides a structure for clear answers to come in meditation, contemplation and prayer through direct dialogue with one's higher self and beings of light.

Through the channelling system, messages arrive from beings such as angels, saints or enlightened masters (sometimes called ascended masters), or from people who have passed over. This book focuses primarily on receiving direct communication from higher beings such as angels or enlightened masters and less on messages from people who have passed over, for this is the role of a medium. Serving as a medium is a worthy path. It can also be a very difficult one. Often people who work as mediums have honed their skills over many lifetimes. They are highly trained to keep strong boundaries when working with the third or fourth dimensional spirits of human beings who have passed over and who still carry unresolved emotion.

The medium's role is very important, often serving as a counsellor to people who have lost someone very close to them and also as a counsellor for the spirits of people who have passed over who are not yet ready to ascend fully into fifth dimensional consciousness. It must also be noted that a medium may also have developed the capacity to communicate with the fifth dimensional manifestation of a deceased person, ascended masters and angelic beings. Their role as an intermediary for third and fourth dimensional spirits does not limit their capacity to also channel fifth dimensional beings and above.

In this book, we bypass the third and fourth dimensional levels though we certainly do not discount the role of a medium. Our work, through this book, focuses on developing conscious connections to beings such as archangels, saints and enlightened masters who have transcended their third and fourth dimensional aspects and have ascended into the fifth dimension. Some ascended masters have incarnated on Earth over many lifetimes in order to reach the levels of compassion and wisdom required to transcend fourth dimensional experience and move into the unconditional love frequency of the fifth dimension. Such beings are extremely helpful to us because their human experience is extensive. Their advice is relevant to one's own experience. They have developed useful systems that assist in the practical task of being human and working to remember and integrate the higher self into the human experience.

The passages ahead provide information about the third, fourth and fifth dimensions so that the initiate may better understand the term 'ascended' or 'enlightened masters' and fifth dimensional beings. This is in order to develop confidence in creating conscious connections to such beings. These passages also outline some of the many beings availabe to assist and the dimension in which they primarily reside. It is the vibrational frequency of the being that determines the dimension in which it primarily resides. All dimensions are divine and the vibrational frequency of beings does not make any being more or less worthy in the eyes of the Divine.

Human beings are designed to ascend to the fifth dimension, but not all beings are charged with this task. Their existence in the dimension of their vibratory rate is entirely appropriate for their function within the All That Is. Indeed there are some beings for whom the third or fourth dimension is their rightful home. They are not 'stuck' or lost when they reside there; rather, they are living in the realm that is their natural home, in the dimension that their realm was designed to exist within.

Spirits of people who have passed on from the Earth's plane are designed to ascend beyond the third and fourth dimensional planes. Spirits who are not yet ready to ascend are not intended to wander aimlessly through the third or fourth dimension trying to gain access to the channelling systems of incarnated humans. They are intended to return to halls and places of light established by the angelic realms until their time comes to reincarnate into the Earth's plane once more and receive another opportunity to raise their vibrational frequency. This is so that they may eventually ascend into the fifth dimension alongside other human incarnates. When one calls upon the Light to clear a lower spirit from one's energy field (as in the Energy Field Clearing Meditation in Part One), the Light removes the spirit from its aimless wanderings or from interfering in the channelling systems of human incarnates. The Light takes the spirit to a hall or place of light overseen by the angelic realms until it is time for it to reincarnate according to the will of its higher councils.

An Outline of the Dimensional Homes of Beings

Below is a basic outline of the different experiences that humans and beings have available as a result of the dimension wherein they choose to reside. There would be no end to the number of beings that could be listed in each section. The beings shown in the 'fifth dimension' section are listed because they are commonly known and may serve to give the reader a broader overview of the concept of dimensional existence. The outline begins in the Middle Third Dimension, as the relevant starting point for understanding dimensions as they relate to channelling.

Middle Third Dimension

Existing at this level are human beings and animals who hold the intent to survive as the primary reason for their actions. These ones view their environment as always potentially hostile and scan other humans or animals for the opportunities these humans or animals provide to enhance their own means of survival. Humans and animals vibrating at this level display highly aggressive behaviour when provoked or attacked, or their young are threatened. Humans in the middle third dimension slaughter animals and eat them without honouring the spirit of the animal that gave its life. These humans will also cut down trees without warning or communicating with the tree being that lives inside. Humans at this vibratory rate can begin to move beyond this level through acknowledging the spirit of the animals, trees and the Earth itself as being crucial to their survival. This acknowledgement eventually brings respect for the natural world and honouring of its spiritual element.

Although the middle third dimension is an appropriate vibratory rate for many members of the animal kingdom, it is not the intended home for human beings. Humans vibrating at this level attack without provocation, can be addicted to substances that fuel their aggression, and assault other human beings, animals and the nature realms for the misguided perception that they will somehow gain personally through doing so.

Upper Third Dimension

While residing in the upper third dimension, the human being is uncomfortable in his life and wants to change himself or his circumstances. He is aware that his own behaviour and/or his life may change by taking certain steps to bring about change. Many human beings who have experienced lifetimes of awakening (or in rare cases, ascension) may incarnate at this level to rapidly clear their own karma or karma that they volunteered to clear before removing the veils and progressing swiftly into the fourth dimension. Often children born with strong wills and intense drives to master skills and learn quickly are already vibrating at this level of dimensional experience. Once these children clear their minimal karma and acquire the necessary skills they move quickly into the fourth dimension.

Humans who remain in this vibratory level even when it is uncomfortable, and who do not recognise the need to commit to moving beyond this level, believe they can manipulate their external world so that they can make themselves more comfortable without having to change internally. Through lifetimes of experiencing this vibratory rate they learn that regardless of how many external changes they make, the key to their contentment comes from accepting that their discomfort is internal. The key to their contentment is also found in choosing to raise their vibrational frequency to allow them access to a higher dimension that is more conducive to their natural state.

Some animals live in this level of dimensional existence, caring for each other and protecting their mates and their young. These animals may live in packs or families and operate in a functional, team-spirited way to support themselves. For such animals, this level of dimensional experience is entirely appropriate and comfortable.

Lower fourth dimension

This level is the first realm within the fourth dimension and akin to a quarter of it in terms of overall size. It is generally experienced by human incarnates and spirits alike as hazy or foggy, where the conscious mind is not yet alert to realms and dimensions beyond the physical plane. It is the initial stage of awakening, where human incarnates or spirits begin to question whether there might just be a realm beyond their current one, however they are not fully convinced of the fact. It is also the realm of spirits who have generally recently passed over and have not yet let go of their earthly life and the physical plane.

Human beings at this level begin to have 'experiences', which entice them to continue with their awakening and investigation of the possibility of higher realms and dimensions of consciousness. They begin to remember another state of being although they cannot yet determine fully what it is that they are remembering. What is happening is that their body cell memory and blueprints are beginning to activate, connecting them to their hierarchies (see 'Definition of Terms' section for a definition of one's hierachy). These vague insights and experiences will make more sense to them when they ascend into higher levels of the fourth dimension.

Some animals and insects live in this level of dimensional existence. They may live in organized colonies and support themselves through their ability to work together. Many amphibians and sea creatures are fourth dimensional and live within different levels of the fourth dimension according to their species.

Middle Fourth Dimension

This level accounts for approximately half of the fourth dimension and the experiences or existence within it tend to fall into two major categories.

First, at this level of dimensional experience, beings are able to carry fear. When humans pass through this level with the intent of moving to the upper fourth dimension, they are aware of their fears and are consciously working to transmute them. They will process vast numbers of aspects using the method that best serves them and they will communicate with the Divine through prayer. This expresses their intention to receive the blessing of the Divine in order to ascend. They realise that their ascension comes through integrating the Divine into their everyday life, however they perceive the Divine to be. In essence, this working relationship with the Divine allows humans to process any aspects of them that are not aligned to Divine Will and enter the state of grace that allows the Divine Will to be done in all matters and circumstances.

In order for one to move into the upper fourth dimension one must vibrate at a vibrational frequency that reflects a level of love and compassion in one's heart, energy field or consciousness. Beings who have not attained sufficient love and compassion for themselves and others will not be able to maintain the vibrational frequency required for elevation into the next level of the fourth dimension.

The second category of experience relates to those who have passed over. If the spirit of a person who has passed over is disruptive, generally it will operate from this level of dimensional existence. At the lower end of the middle fourth dimension, spirits have realised that they are in a realm beyond the Earth plane, but may still carry unresolved emotions and fears from their lifetimes on Earth. Occasionally however there are disruptive spirits, who have honed their skills or gained the psychic power available in the fourth dimension, able to operate at the higher end of the middle fourth dimension. These spirits are not able to access power above the middle fourth dimension because their intent to manipulate and cause harm keeps their vibrational frequency in the middle fourth dimension.

Upper fourth dimension

The upper fourth dimension is technically the final quarter of the fourth dimension and is the most common vibratory rate for human beings who have awakened, who remember their higher assignments and reason for their time on Earth, but have not yet ascended completely. They are in the process of ascending, of clearing lower emotion, thoughts and aspects of themselves. They are consciously taking responsibility for their incarnation on Earth through their meetings and conscious communication with the higher realms. Initiates who have awakened and hold the vibrational frequency of this level within their physical bodies may interact consciously with nature beings, angelic beings of Earth and the nature realms, regularly communicating with their higher selves and higher councils.

Fourth – Fifth Dimensional Gateway

This gateway level exists to accommodate ascended masters in training or human incarnates at the final stage before full enlightenment. It also serves these masters on their path to full enlightenment to retain their connection to the fourth dimension, and where relevant, maintain their physical body, in order to facilitate their Earth assignment. Other being at this level include:

Tree beings

Over-lighting devas or spirits of many plants

Fifth Dimension

In the fifth dimension, beings are automatically aligned to the will of the Divine as a function of their fifth dimensional positioning. There is no duality of 'good and bad' in this dimension, as everything within the dimension's vibratory rate is aligned to the universal principle of harmony. Fear cannot visit or reside in this realm. Fear exists at a lower vibrational frequency than the fifth dimension, rendering its co-existence technically impossible. The vibrational frequency of the fifth dimension cancels out and automatically transmutes the frequency of fear. The fifth dimension operates naturally within the boundary of the principles of harmony and the law known as 'the Law of One', which in practical terms recognises the interconnectedness of all creation.

The beings listed below operate in the fifth dimension. There are many more beings who belong to this list, too innumerable to mention here. In some instances, the beings listed as residing in the fifth dimension may do so in order to facilitate their assignments on Earth although their true home bases may be in the sixth or seventh dimensions or beyond.

Archangel Michael

Archangel Raphael

Archangel Gabriel

Archangel Uriel

Lord Jesus

Mother Mary

Saint Germain

Lord Buddha

The Office of the Law of One

The High Council of the Spiritual Hierarchy for Earth (explained below in more detail)

All beings listed here and many more, sit on the High Council of the Spiritual Hierarchy for Earth.

When one chooses to channel fully enlightened masters and archangels one ensures that the being who comes to one's aid vibrates at the fifth dimensional level, abiding by the Law of One, which says: "When all are allowed to be in their frequencies all shall come into peace and into harmony". The Law of One is a very important key particularly when one wishes to channel beings. When one channels beings from the fifth dimension, one automatically channels beings who abide by the Law of One. Such beings have humanity's highest benefit at heart and have proven themselves to be worthy of assisting humanity at the highest level.

As one connects to the fifth dimension and accesses one's fifth dimensional channelling system, one raises the vibrational frequency of one's energy field so that one naturally ascends. Channelling becomes a type of spiritual path in so far as it provides a path that supports ascension. In order for the channelling path to also facilitate the ascension path, one must align to the fifth dimension and choose to channel fifth dimensional beings working for the

Spiritual Hierarchy for Earth on assignments designed and intended to serve humanity's highest benefit.

The Dimensions and the Chakra System

The chakras, or main energy centres in the body, hold the vibrational frequencies of the dimensional level with which they are compatible. In a human who resonates with the third dimension, the middle third dimension connects into his base chakra. The upper third dimension may connect into his base or sacral chakra depending on his evolution. When he chooses to awaken and ascend, he will transcend the third dimension and his chakras will release third dimensional frequencies, assisting him with his passage to the fourth dimension. Eventually, as he progresses through the levels of dimensional experience, he will ascend into the fifth dimension.

Diagram of a Non-Awakened Human Being

BROW CHAKRA
(Fourth-fifth dimensional gateway level) The potential exists to access the fourth-fifth dimensional gateway through this chakra, but the access point lies dormant.

HEART CHAKRA
(Middle fourth dimensional level) The potential to heal past pain and open one's heart remains ever-present even when this level is dormant.

SACRAL CHAKRA
(Upper third dimensional level) The human draws strength, but also fear from this level and looks to the world for stimulus and ideas about what he can have and what he should want. He takes from the material world.

BASE CHAKRA
(Middle third dimensional level) The human defends and strikes as his instincts compel him. He is unaware of the energy he projects outwardly and unaware of how it returns to him.

CROWN CHAKRA
Fifth dimensional potential, but potential lies dormant.

THROAT CHAKRA
(Upper fourth dimensional level) The potential to discover, live and express one's highest potential in the upper fourth dimension and physical plane simultaneously is present, but lies dormant.

SOLAR PLEXUS CHAKRA
(Lower fourth dimensional level) The human may glimpse this level and access his emotional centre although full understanding of his feelings will be unclear as will be his ability to perceive his higher mind.

KEY

He is oblivious to these levels and thus they lie dormant.

Awareness at this level is fleeting.

The human operates from the sacral and base chakras.

Chakra Ascension Exercise for the Awakened and Ascending Human

As the chakras are involved in the process of awakening and ascension, the following exercise is offered as a key for opening portals to the crown and brow chakras which have a vital role in channelling.

Enter meditation. Close your eyes and focus on your breath flowing in and out of your body.

Feel the area at the top of your head, the crown chakra. Feel the energy moving, possibly circling, around this energy centre. Ask your crown chakra to awaken to its highest potential now. Ask it to prepare for ascension into a fifth dimensional energy vortex and to allow itself to be a receptacle for the fifth dimensional energy to flow through your body and charge the rest of your chakras.

Visualise or sense this fifth dimensional energy filling your crown and flowing through your crown into the space between your two eyes, your third eye or brow chakra. Ask your brow chakra to awaken completely to its highest potential and ascend. Feel the fifth dimensional energy filling your brow, transmuting limitations or blockages. With your eyes closed visualise yourself stepping through a door inside your third eye and out into a vast blue sky. You gaze across the vista before you and feel the full expansiveness of your etheric sight. You are no longer confined to the limitations of the physical plane. You can see all that you need to see.

As you hover in this sky-like realm, visualise your entire body in this upper fourth dimensional level. See all the chakras of your body release the shackles of lower dimensional experience and shine with the vibrational frequency of this higher level. Tell your body and its chakras that it is now time to ascend.

Return from meditation, allowing the full power of this awareness to integrate into your body.

Basic Outline of the Spiritual Hierarchy for Earth and its Offices

The Spiritual Hierarchy for Earth is vast. It is a massive structure of sound, colour, light and frequency that houses the human race and all other realms and species that are the true inheritors of planet Earth. Although its core governing body sits in the fifth dimension, it has the ability to exist and hold its presence in all dimensions. Numerous offices and councils exist within the Spiritual Hierarchy for Earth. Some of these offices are held by beings who sit in councils for a term, others are permanent members of an office or a council and will hold these positions for as long as the Spiritual Hierarchy for Earth exists.

The Spiritual Hierarchy for Earth consists of twelve founding hierarchies that have worked together since the formation of the blueprint for planet Earth. These twelve hierarchies are also part of the same spiritual family, joined together since the time before time. At the centre of this spiritual family is the Great Central Sun, the Christ Light of this universe, perfectly balanced in its masculine and feminine aspects. The Spiritual Hierarchy for Earth is a structure with a specific function to serve Earth and all beings who co-exist on Earth. It consists of offices held by individual hierarchies, specific beings within those hierarchies, and jointly held offices. Jointly held offices have councils where every member of the office holds a seat. Offices within the Spiritual Hierarchy for Earth hold the fourth and fifth dimensional frequencies for the beings, human incarnates and frequency bands that they represent.

There are vast numbers of offices within the Spiritual Hierarchy for Earth and there are thousands of beings and human incarnates who work within and actively assist the offices. As one reads through the list below, one may receive a powerful sense of the office or offices one serves through one's human incarnation. Some of the major governing councils and offices are listed below:

The Office of Family

All hierarchies belonging to the wider spiritual family also belong to the Office of Family and contribute their unique frequencies to the office. The office seeks to harmonise the energy between the hierarchies, which in turn helps to harmonise the space between family members on Earth. The office oversees the healing of ancient rifts between the hierarchies of the spiritual family by organizing for members of each hierarchy to incarnate into family clusters together. As these human incarnates work through the issues that arise in their human lives, they assist to harmonise the energy and clear karmic debt between members of the spiritual family.

As well as harmonizing the energy between existing family frequencies on Earth, the office seeks to integrate higher family frequencies on Earth. For families that choose to accept these higher frequencies, it is possible for all members to ascend together into the early stages of fifth dimensional experience.

Office of Children

The Office of Children oversees the development of 'the child' and the experience of 'childhood'. This office is the keeper of the sacred keys known as the Innocence of Childhood. Divine beings who sit in this office made an agreement many thousands of years ago to incarnate on Earth and remain intensely incarnated in human bodies until every child experienced peace, and true Innocence of Childhood, as childhood was designed originally to be.

Some souls use childhood to process karmic debt or work through voluntary karma. For these souls, peace and the Innocence of Childhood must still be presented, however fleetingly, so that the soul knows the right path and the highest truth. Beings who sit in the Office of Children work tirelessly to present the keys of peace and the Innocence of Childhood, and represent them well, to all children. This is done primarily through human contact, for example an Office of Children representative appears in a child's life for a period of time (teacher, nurse, aid worker etc) or as a permanent figure (community elder, family member, neighbour, family friend). In cases where an incarnated representative cannot reach a certain child, the child will receive a dream or visitation from a member of the Office of Children. The Office of Children uses educational means to present its keys to children such as working through its human incarnated members who are writers and illustrators, to install representations of the keys in children's stories and books.

Office of Youth

The Office of Youth oversees the adolescent phase. The adolescent phase acts as a transitional plane from childhood to adulthood, and offers a vital opportunity to grow and expand, and for the soul to seek oneself and find oneself, or to find the path that leads to oneself. The Office of Youth was established to present the key to one's path. Light-workers working for this office do so in various capacities in order to present vital keys to adolescents so that they fulfil their highest purpose on Earth by first recognising their own path and choosing to step onto it. These light-workers may work in various professions e.g. as teachers, scout leaders, chaplains, counsellors, coaches and community leaders. They may also serve as biological mothers and fathers, and people who nurture children and young people as their non-biological parents, guardians and caregivers.

Office of Women

The Office of Women exists to assist every human incarnated female to reach her highest potential as a woman on Earth. The Office of Women oversees the development and ascension of the feminine energy on Earth, and the integration of higher feminine frequencies into Earth's collective consciousness and emotional body.

Office of Men

The Office of Men ensures that higher masculine frequencies integrate into the consciousness of mankind. The Office of Men oversees the gradual ascension of male awareness on Earth.

Office of Animals

The Office of Animals was responsible for the integration of animal species on Earth. It oversees and records the experiences of the species, how they interact with Earth, how they evolve and in some cases, the office assists species to take their experience and re-integrate back into their own planetary worlds and kingdoms, sometimes away from planet Earth.

Working for the Spiritual Hierarchy for Earth

Channels working for the Spiritual Hierarchy for Earth may serve specific assignments within the offices mentioned above or other offices not listed, as they are multiple and highly specific. Channels working on such assignments receive direct instructions from the offices or from the beings who serve in the offices. These instructions are received through the channelling system through the medium of thought-transference telepathic channelling and/or automatic writing. Some human incarnates may also receive instructions through their intuition and thus serve the offices intuitively and as their compassionate hearts guide them.

The role of a channel working for the Spiritual Hierarchy for Earth is very different to the role of a psychic or medium. When one works for the Spiritual Hierarchy for Earth specifically as a channel, although one may be naturally psychic, one is not using psychic ability, but is surrendering completely to Divine Will and all spiritual councils aligned to that frequency. In order to work as a genuine channel for the Spiritual Hierarchy for Earth, one must be aligned to the Law of One. This alignment offers the channel protection. The spiritual councils working in alignment with the Law of One do not misuse their volunteers. One is instead in a balanced, health-promoting, team-like arrangement. One should not become worn out, overrun by an external force or will, or disadvantaged in any way. If one is in a channelling arrangement with beings where one feels this way, one is not channelling the Spiritual Hierarchy for Earth. The Spiritual Hierarchy for Earth is aligned to the highest benefit of all and any person working as a genuine channel for this hierarchy experiences abundance and love, and never the opposite.

Only those who are properly trained can channel as a representative for the Spiritual Hierarchy for Earth consistently for themselves and others. There are two important points in this statement that must be clearly understood. In the first instance, although one must be properly trained before working as a channel for the Spiritual Hierarchy for Earth, there are instances where initiates awakened to channelling this lifetime without undergoing any training. For these ones, their training occurred in their past incarnations or they incarnated directly from a dimensional frequency where training was not necessary due to their automatic alignment to their higher assignments.

Secondly the term 'properly trained' is not used in the traditional sense and does not imply that one must attend a formal course or gain a certificate of completion of some sort. In order to receive the training at this time on

Earth, one does not need to pay another person or be offered a qualification by an institution on Earth. One's highest training comes directly from within one's own hierarchy and high council before being approved by the Spiritual Hierarchy for Earth. Only those who dedicate themselves to the task of clearing away the debris within themselves, qualify to receive high frequency channelling systems from the spiritual councils.

This selection process is not based on elitism, but is instead based upon the right and proper intention being held before power is given. One cannot receive these types of channelling systems any other way. They are bestowed upon human initiates by the spiritual councils and not by any human being or spiritual institution in the physical plane. Never believe that another teacher or channel has the ability to open or close one's channels. This is done only through the work one does for oneself and in conjunction with the higher councils of one's hierarchy.

Through aligning one's will to Divine Will, one fulfils the necessary function required to qualify as a channel for the Spiritual Hierarchy for Earth. In order to feel truly comfortable with the notion of aligning, a more in-depth understanding of alignment to the fifth dimension and Divine Will can be gained through studying the sections below that provide further details about the High Council of the Law of One and in particular, its administrator Archangel Michael.

Divine Will and the High Council of the Law of One

The Spiritual Hierarchy for Earth established a governing council, the High Council of the Law of One, to determine right and true action aligned to Divine Will and also to determine any actions that were against the highest benefit of the All That Is. This council was established to serve the Spiritual Hierarchy for Earth and all actions and decisions made on Earth. It also serves other councils beyond Earth that are not relevant to the Earth assignment. It is an independent body not aligned to the will of any one hierarchy, but sits in its home base, in a frequency band in the upper levels of the fifth dimension, close in frequency to the Office of the Christ.

The Prime Governor of the High Council of the Law of One is Archangel Michael. He works closely with other beings of light who have served the

High Council of the Law of One for thousands of years. These beings include archangels of the highest level of integrity: Archangel Raphael, Archangel Gabriel and Archangel Uriel.

Scores of beings from the angelic councils work to instill the principles of the Law of One council throughout this universe. These angelic beings work tirelessly to answer the calls of beings who have strayed from the light and now choose to return home. The angelic beings offer their protection, support and compassion to renegade beings as they break negative alliances and confront parts of themselves that walked away from their alignment to Divine Will. The angelic beings work with the Office of the Christ to ensure that when a renegade being surrenders its fear and its activity against the High Council of the Law of One, it receives the healing it needs in order to return home to the love of itself. In addition to the angelic beings, there are many other beings working in direct service to the High Council of the Law of One to ensure its principles are applied across the universe for the good of all.

The High Council of the Law of One judges the decisions made by all hierarchies and council members within the Spiritual Hierarchy for Earth and categorises them depending upon their intent and their impact on other hierarchies. The majority of decisions made are left 'un-judged' for the decision is automatically aligned to Divine Will. There is no need to question or investigate decisions that align to the Will of God, for by the nature of their alignment, they automatically benefit the highest good and will of all within the All That Is.

The High Council of the Law of One investigates decisions when another hierarchy or Spiritual Hierarchy for Earth council member raises a complaint and/or when the Law of One council detects a disruption to the natural harmony of the universal frequencies, indeed a 'disturbance in the force'. When a 'disturbance in the force' is detected, the council moves swiftly to determine the nature of the decision made that created the disturbance, identifying who made it and what the intention was behind the decision. Intention is considered of the utmost importance to the High Council of the Law of One, and decisions are categorized based on the intention behind the decision. This differentiates between mistakes, fearful, frustrated, and aggressive behaviour, decisions made by those who are deeply pained, lonely and/or isolated, and renegade activity. Ultimately it is the key to Wisdom and Compassion, held by the Central Sun Hierarchy, that balances the decisions of the High Council of the Law of One.

Every human being at some point has lashed out in anger or harboured thoughts and said words to hurt and punish another or themselves – and yet human beings also have within them the power to repair the past and restore the present. For example, by returning to one's past life memories of Atlantis, Lemuria, Egypt and so on, one might discover a part of oneself which chose to do things that one now finds chastening. Understand that in those times, beings found it difficult to remain upon Earth and always see clearly the highest path to take. One must not judge these parts of oneself, for often they remain abandoned and unaccounted for because they fear judgment from the higher councils. Such a higher council is within oneself and in one's hierarchy, and thus is it one's task to lovingly restore these aspects. Welcome them home so that their time lost in the desert of their own fear and loneliness can end forevermore. This is achieved through aligning to Divine Will.

Before beginning the following exercise, spend some time with the diagram 'Your Hierarchy' (see 'Definition of Terms' section) and meditate upon its image, until the structure of the hierarchy is familiar. For further clarification, refer to the 'Channelling System' diagram on page 46 to see how the fifth dimensional energy is able to flow through you from above and below.

Alignment to Divine Will Exercise

As one prepares to connect to the channelling system, the following exercise will help to ensure one is aligned to Divine Will which is crucial to one's role/work as a channel.

Sit quietly and enter meditation.

Call forth Archangel Michael to enter your meditation space.

One must enter one's heart to awaken the presence of Divine Will from within oneself. Every person's heart contains this eternal presence. Breathe deeply to enter your heart's chamber.

(If you struggle to feel the presence of Divine Will within, ask Archangel Michael to touch your heart. His touch will reawaken your conscious connection to the ever-present Divine Will).

Once the awareness of this presence is activated, visualise your hierarchy as a structure of light encompassing your body and extending above your head, into the realms above, until you sense or see the Divine Source and golden light of the fifth dimensional levels of your hierarchy.

Call every level of your hierarchy, from your aspects in the earth/physical plane to your fourth dimensional aspects to awaken and connect to the presence of Divine Will within and call every aspect to align to Divine Will completely without reservation.

You will sense when this alignment is complete.

In the case of blocking aspects, when you sense that something is not aligned, despite completing the 'Alignment Exercise', call forth the non-aligned aspect as in the Aspect Therapy Meditation (found in Part Three of this book). Once the non-aligned aspect and its reason for not aligning is identified through communicating with it in meditation, call forth Archangel Michael's assistance to awaken its conscious connection to the ever-present Divine Will within.

Understanding Archangel Michael's Service

In order to develop full faith and trust in Archangel Michael as a partner and fellow worker in the healing room or channelling session, one must first understand the truth of this most ancient being of light. Archangel Michael carries this title while in service to the angelic kingdoms of light, aligned to the Law of One. The Christ Michael is a higher aspect of Archangel Michael in service to the universe that contains all universes. The Christ Michael is the highest level of the Central Sun hierarchy that can be perceived by the human mind at this time and is the unification of the two aspects of the Central Sun, Wisdom and Compassion, indeed the Central Sun hierarchy balanced within its masculine and feminine aspects. Michael carries wisdom of the highest degree to all matters within the universes. Christ carries the heart of compassion, applying the compassionate healing presence of the Divine to all matters. Christ Michael carries the balance of Wisdom and Compassion to all matters within this universe and all universes.

Archangel Michael has led entire realms that strayed from Harmony home to the light and home to His Father through incarnating into the realm as a being who is not of the realm, but sympathetic to its reality and experience. His strategy, teachings, example, and clear guidelines have allowed the beings of different realms a clear path to follow so that their way home is obvious. This procedure has been repeated through the direct incarnation of the Christ child into human form upon Earth's floor. Other members of the Central Sun hierarchy have also incarnated in similar ways to assist the human being to recognise his ability to return Home.

In the past, over many thousands of years, Archangel Michael has come to the aid of many, many beings who have called upon him for assistance and strength to see clearly and recognise at all times and in all of their choices and decisions, the highest path to benefit the Divine in all. Across all time and every tradition, Archangel Michael has restored the sight of souls whose spiritual vision had been temporarily blinded. He has healed the pain in the hearts of those souls who had temporarily doubted the power and the eternal sovereignty of the Divine. His commitment to maintaining his presence in this part of the universe, and specifically Earth, has never once wavered. His commitment to each individual light-worker on Earth is as strong as it is to each realm, kingdom, and species that he has pledged to oversee and protect.

Once one feels comfortable with the integrity of the Spiritual Hierarchy for Earth, its governing principle, the Law of One, its administrators, Archangel Michael and the High Council of the Law of One, one can begin confidently to open one's channelling system, readying oneself for service as a channel for the Spiritual Hierarchy for Earth.

The Mechanics of the Channelling System

The channelling system sits in the crown chakra, at the top of the head and connects directly into the Higher Self and Incarnation Team level of the hierarchy (see 'Definition of Terms' section for detailed explanation of Higher Self and Incarnation Team level). In the physical body, it connects from the crown chakra through to the soles of the feet and then to the earth-star, which is the anchor point in the Earth that serves to connect the human body to the Earth. The channelling system uses the meridians in the body to connect from the crown to the feet, with the meridians acting as a physical conduit. Every channelling system is assigned a Gateway Guardian who filters and to a certain extent controls the channelling system gateways that sit in the crown chakra and in the soles of the feet. This protects the physical vehicle – the human body – from incompatible frequencies.

Diagram of the Channelling System

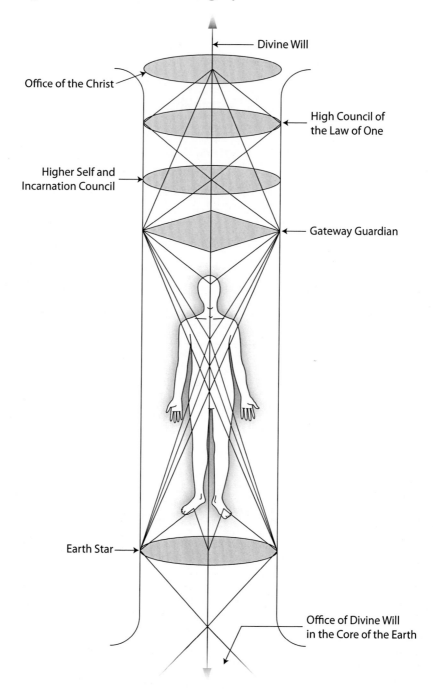

Meeting the Gateway Guardian of One's Channelling System

Through clearing the energy field on a daily basis using the exercises from Part One or another program, over the space of a week one becomes more aware of the energies flowing through the body and energies flowing all around the energy field. Over several months, one becomes more aware of external thoughts and their impact on how one feels about oneself. One begins to recognise the thoughts that are one's own and the thoughts that are not. After reclaiming ownership over the mind it is possible to distinguish the difference between true thoughts, originating from oneself or the higher realms, and lower thoughts projected by others or circling through the global mind.

Once one is 'at the wheel' of one's mind, the beings of light ready to support one's evolution into working as a channel, present themselves. These beings of light are members of the spiritual family and serve in the Spiritual Hierarchy for Earth. Beings of light working in the Spiritual Hierarchy for Earth and working on the Earth assignment, are available to communicate messages through channels to human incarnates. They reside in the fifth dimension although they have the capacity to work within many dimensional planes. By channelling these beings over a period of time, the channel comes to understand them and develop relationships with them.

When the initiate wishes to access higher guidance for her and others and open her channelling system, she is assigned a being who has volunteered to serve as a Gateway Guardian and holds the admission key for other beings from the fifth dimension wishing to connect with the human initiate. A Gateway Guardian chooses to assist human incarnates to open their channels. Unlike other beings of light who serve in different roles such as overseeing blueprints, working as divine messengers to bring forth higher levels of information to spiritually awaken humans, the Gateway Guardian serves as the guardian of the channelling system.

Gateway Guardians are generally fifth dimensional beings who sit in the fifth dimension, but have the ability to connect to all other dimensions of experience. They are aligned automatically to the Law of One and because of this alignment the channel can trust that the Gateway Guardian is always serving the highest good and Divine Will. And in every case, they are always accompanied by Archangel Michael in their first visitation to the human initiate, so that one might think of this functioning as an introductory service of the highest order.

Meditation is a direct way to connect to one's own Gateway Guardian, facilitating the passage through the third and fourth dimensions to connect into the fifth dimension. The passage through the third and fourth dimensions may manifest in meditation as unfamiliar, lower spirits or beings presenting themselves to connect into one's channelling system. In the meditation outlined ahead, one is aided to bypass these beings, to resist forming any connection with these beings, and to move through to the higher levels, connecting with the fifth dimension and with one's true Gateway Guardian.

There are many channels who choose to channel third and fourth dimensional beings. In many ways it is an arduous path, though it is a path that may bring resolution for those beings and for the people who are receiving the messages. Generally, and especially while in training to channel, it is safer to bypass these third and fourth dimensional beings as due to their residence in the third or fourth dimension they are likely to harbor unresolved aspects and emotions that are compatible with the vibrational frequency of their dimension and may obstruct the service one aspires to provide.

In the following meditation, after entering the quiet space within, one's Gateway Guardian will arrive to assist with connection into the fifth dimension. Initially, in this space, other beings may appear who are not one's Gateway Guardian. These beings may cause confusion and their faces may change, making it difficult to focus clearly. The first thing to do in this instance is to shine light on such beings causing them to dissipate. If they dissolve, one knows immediately that the being/s were third and fourth dimensional. A true fifth dimensional being can stand in the light that one shines on it. By using Divine Light to shine upon unfamiliar beings and calling forth Archangel Michael, one is able to swiftly discern lower beings from a Gateway Guardian.

Archangel Michael as one's additional guardian and protector is able to transmute any lower vibrational beings and spirits who choose not to serve one's highest good and will. When entering into meditation call forth Divine Light to shine down upon the beings who present, and also call forth

Archangel Michael to stand next to the being who presents as one's Gateway Guardian. If this being cannot stand in Archangel Michael's light and cannot stand tall under his full gaze, accepting the full power of the Divine Light within its presence, then one knows that this being is not one's Gateway Guardian. The spirit that dissolves under Archangel Michael's gaze is likely to be from the third or fourth dimension, or specifically, the astral plane. It is of the utmost importance to pass through the astral plane, through the lower levels of the etheric, which is also the lower level of the fourth dimension. One must set one's sights on breaking through into the upper levels of the fourth dimension, which act as a gateway to the fifth dimension, so that one can then connect to the beings of light who are of that level of integrity.

A fifth dimensional being is aligned to the Law of One and is committed to one's highest interest and the highest interest of the people whom one assists through channelling. A Gateway Guardian has all of these elements and is assigned by the high councils to act as one's teacher and guard through the channelling process. Through working with one's Gateway Guardian, one may receive the Gateway Guardian's name, either in the first meditation, or over the days and weeks ahead. For some people, receiving the name is not important. For others, it helps them develop a relationship with their Gateway Guardian.

One's only concern is whether the beings can stand next to Archangel Michael, regardless of what they look like or where they originate. One must apply this test to all beings who present themselves. The being must be able to stand in front of Archangel Michael regardless of what the being says or how one feels about this being. This is particularly important if a relative comes as a Gateway Guardian because although one may know the relative, trust the relative or have an emotional connection with the relative, the relative may not necessarily be one's Gateway Guardian. If a relative who has passed over appears, it is still important that one asks this relative to stand next to Archangel Michael and be tested. At another time, one may choose to go back and communicate with the relative, but it is more important at the moment to establish a proper connection to the Gateway Guardian rather than be distracted by other beings. If the relative, when standing in front of Archangel Michael, moves away, it is simply because the relative is not the chosen Gateway Guardian. Again, one can communicate with the relative at a later stage, but do establish a firm connection with the Gateway Guardian first.

The Gateway Guardian protects the initiate's channelling system from spirits in the 'otherworld' and other human beings where protection is required. On rare occasions, a client seeking channelling may not have the channel's highest interest at heart. This doesn't mean the client has negative plans for the channel, but they may have a clear agenda about what they want to get out of the session. They may want information that suits what they want to hear or what they want to happen. Their projections onto the channel's energy field can become so strong that the channel struggles to hear clearly or to receive the messages from the Gateway Guardian.

In these instances, it is very important that one feels secure in one's relationship with one's Gateway Guardian, so that if one is not feeling confident about the session, one can stop, connect into one's Gateway Guardian and ask for advice. For this reason, it is important in these initial stages to spend time establishing a relationship with one's Gateway Guardian. Like all relationships, it requires time and commitment to build up a steady rapport, but the rewards make it worthwhile. Regardless of what other people are asking or the reasons they have come for channelling, one will be safe-guarded knowing one has learnt to always trust one's relationship with one's Gateway Guardian. Through a well-developed connection to her Gateway Guardian, the initiate carves a pathway that is safe and protected.

Gateway Guardian Meditation

Prepare to enter into meditation. Sit quietly, closing your eyes and relaxing the body through breathing steadily.

Call forth Archangel Michael. Feel the presence of this great being of light. Feel the presence of Archangel Michael in the room.

Visualise a place of safety. This may be a place that you have visited physically before or it may be or a place that appears in your mind.

Sit in this place of safety and see or sense Archangel Michael standing close by. Sense the light around Archangel Michael, feeling his light permeate the entire vicinity and his loving support and true commitment to the Divine.

Now become aware and watch as another being walks into the place of safety. As this being draws closer, sense whether this being chooses to appear male or female, or of no clear sex. Sense the color and the type of the being's clothing. This being will now stand beside Archangel Michael.

Ask Archangel Michael to shine light on this being so that its identity as your true gateway guardian can be revealed. Divine Light will shine on this being.

Allow Archangel Michael's light to intensify and shine through this being, highlighting the entire length of its form. If this being remains present, stands firm and possibly intensifies the light, you will know this being to be your Gateway Guardian. If the being dissolves or moves away, do not be concerned. This is a positive sign for you have consciously passed through the astral plane and the lower level of the fourth dimension. Now call forth the Gateway Guardian and allow the next being to present. Again, ask Archangel Michael to shine light on this new being. If this being stays present and in many ways its light intensifies, this being is your true Gateway Guardian. If, like the first being, it dissolves or moves away, do not be concerned and repeat the process.

Once you are confident that this being of light is your Gateway

Guardian and you feel or see the light of this being shining and the love from this being entering into your heart, open a channel of communication with this being by consciously asking it if it has any messages.

Take some time to listen to this being, to receive any insights, feelings or messages, possibly even a name for this being. You have shared ancient history with your Gateway Guardian, having worked together in other incarnations. This being is also part of your spiritual family. Take some time now to remember.

Send love from your heart into the heart of your Gateway Guardian and feel this exchange of energy intensifying. Focus now on the area between your eyes. This is your third eye or brow chakra. Feel your third eye exchange energy with your Gateway Guardian so that a firm telepathic connection is established. This allows you to receive a form of channelling that is known as instant perception. It is the ability to perceive the highest perspective and a higher answer from your Gateway Guardian immediately without entering into meditation. As you think a question the answer can appear immediately in your mind.

Ask the Gateway Guardian for any messages that may strengthen your relationship and channels to your Gateway Guardian. Try to remember the answer and write it down after the meditation.

Thank the Gateway Guardian, feeling gratitude and thankfulness and now return from meditation. Write down any messages received.

Over the next week, it is important to meditate to connect to the Gateway Guardian at least once a day. Through connecting with one's Gateway Guardian every day, one strengthens the channels of communication. Like a drainpipe clogged with leaves because it has not been used for some time, a channelling system that has laid dormant for many years, or even lifetimes, can be clogged. When water is poured down a drainpipe, eventually, even if it first begins as a trickle, the leaves flush away until the drain runs clear. A channelling system is very similar. The more one uses channels as in the above meditation the stronger the channels become. Keeping one's house and energy field cleansed is vital while establishing the channelling system. It is important to check through meditation every couple of days that debris has not entered the energy field.

Occasionally the channelling system will be temporarily limited or affected by a phase called 'the natural cycle of rest'. All channels at various times in their lives move through natural cycles of rest, where their channelling system is taking a rest or a break. These cycles unfold differently for each channel. Some experience it as a complete lack of desire to connect spiritually, to meditate or to ask questions of themselves or the higher realms. Others experience this time as one of total focus on the physical life brought about by unavoidable circumstances such as caring for a new baby, an unwell relative, providing for the family, or clearing up after a disaster of some form, where one can allocate very little time for spiritual contemplation.

Beings of light never fatigue their human initiate, and therefore if the channel is physically, mentally or emotionally exhausted, the beings will appear to step away. The higher realms never abandon their human initiate, but will stand in the background until an appropriate time arises to make their presence felt again.

One's connection never completely disappears during the natural cycle of rest. One's channels simply lie dormant until the cycle turns again, and it is time to awaken once more. For many initiates, the natural cycle of rest can feel like a long, dark, lonely night, and is sometimes referred to as 'the dark night of the soul'.

All initiates experience an uplifting side as well as a shadow side of awakening. During the uplifting side of awakening, the initiate experiences an increased feeling of connection, increased psychic ability, stronger and clearer channelled messages, feelings of safety, security and confidence, feelings of self-empowerment, feelings of deep happiness, contentment and bliss and many 'ah ha' moments. During the shadow side of awakening, the initiate can feel overwhelming self-doubt, fear and suspicion as unresolved aspects activate. Though they may be unwelcome at first, they now present as great opportunities for healing. Other manifestations of the shadow side include physical tiredness, headaches, cold/flu like symptoms, anger, the unconscious desire to blame or rebel, as well as self-sabotaging behaviour such as returning to old addictions and finding fault with one's spiritual teacher or higher councils. There may also be an urge to create drama and chaos, to fight with one's spouse, friend or work associate, and in extreme cases to precipitate an accident of some sort.

The dark night of the soul becomes a significantly shorter, less painful journey when the initiate chooses to take responsibility for keeping the energy field clear of debris and addressing unresolved aspects as they arise. In the following chapter, one will receive knowledge and support to heal unresolved aspects and in the process find a profound new measure of acceptance and contentment. For if one of the aims of becoming a channel is to provide service for others, surely one of the greatest blessings is the personal sense of joy and peace one acquires through the steps taken to fulfil the role and the benefits that accrue along the way.

Fine-Tuning the Channelling System

There are two main areas, that once understood and addressed, allow for the proper function of the channelling system for human beings who in this role must be anchored in physical reality.

Area One – The Bridge between the Crown Chakra and Higher Self and Incarnation Team Level

When activating conscious awareness of the channelling system the channel may detect blockages in the free flow of energy between the Higher Self and Incarnation Team level and the crown chakra in the physical body as this is the area most vulnerable to the affects of lower energies and debris. A human incarnate can strengthen the channelling system bridge between the Higher Self and Incarnation Team and crown chakra by meditating on a clear stream of light flowing from the top of the hierarchy, through the Higher Self and Incarnation Team level, through the human body, into the earth-star and into the Office of Divine Will.

The suggestions below will help to cleanse the bridge between the crown chakra and Higher Self and Incarnation Team Level, and thereby allow for fine-tuning of the channelling system:

> Use a smudge stick to cleanse lower entities or spirits attempting to interfere with the bridge that is Area One.

> Soak in an Epsom salt bath with lavender oil and crystals to clear the fourth dimensional levels of the energy field or alternatively, swim in the sea/ocean.

Through meditation, one may detect specific pockets where the energy is not flowing well. Each area can be strengthened individually. Do the Aspect Therapy Meditation to check if there are aspects of one's self restricting or blocking the bridge. Ask in meditation for any blocking aspects to come forth and discuss their fears so that they may be set free.

Area Two – The Physical body

The physical body extends from the crown/top of one's head, to the physical soles of one's feet. This area is usually restricted or blocked due to stagnant energy (energy not coursing through the body easily), or through poorly distributed energy – energy build up in some areas, leaving other areas 'starved' of energy. This lack of proper distribution of energy or energy moving sluggishly creates limitation in the channelling system, which requires the right movement of energy to allow telepathic messages to flow through the physical body from above and below – from the celestial realms and the Earth realms.

While living in the physical plane, the physical body is relevant to the full operation of one's channelling system. There are simple principles that govern the health of the physical body and therefore the proper functioning of the channelling system. The physical body requires all that nature provides in order to be healthy. Through integrating and working in harmony with nature, the physical body receives the sustenance it requires. Individuals who are at odds with nature or try to remove nature from the equation will struggle to fine-tune their channelling system. One can operate a rudimentary channelling system without much involvement or relationship with nature, but in order to ascend into a highly attuned channelling system that is perfectly connected to every level of the physical body and the realms above Earth and within Earth, one must be aware of nature, connected to her internal heartbeat, and aligned to the Office of Divine Will, that rests in the core of Earth.

There are immense rewards in continually refining and fine-tuning the channelling system for as one's connection with the higher realms expands, so too might the number of beings who present themselves, bringing one even greater resources upon which to draw in one's channelling service for others. Like Archangel Michael 'introduced' one's Gateway Guardian to the fold, so might one's Gateway Guardian shepherd in other beings who may serve as spiritual guides, offering additional information to aid the channelling session where appropriate.

PART THREE

Clearing Personal Limitation

Achieving Inner Harmony Through Unifying Aspects of One's Self

Although it has been stated already within these pages, it is worth repeating: for a channelling system to operate at its highest potential, one needs to keep the lines of communication as clear as possible. This requires attention, diligence and regular maintenance, such as following the exercises suggested thus far. For example, the previous chapters of this book have examined debris from others that may block an initiate's ability to connect with the fifth dimensional levels of his own channels and the higher perspective of the higher realms. Through using the Energy Field Clearing Meditation, one has addressed external factors that restrict the flow of clear information from one's Gateway Guardian and consciously cleared debris from the energy field.

The next stage is to look at personal aspects that may block one's channelling system or limit the quality and integrity of the messages received. This work is called Aspect Therapy because its focus is resolving unresolved parts of oneself. These parts, or aspects, may have been splintered off, hidden away or forgotten. When these parts are segregated because they harbour belief systems that cause suffering or harbor emotions that have not been resolved, they become aspects, which hold the vibrational frequency of the energy field at a lower level, holding an initiate in the third or lower fourth dimension.

Unresolved aspects may come from childhood, past lives or they may be projected aspects of other people. Projections from other people in the form of negative thoughts have been addressed in Part One, however it is possible that some aspects sitting in one's energy field may not actually be one's own, but are entities from other people. The Aspect Therapy Meditation outlined below clears these entities in the same way one would clear one's own aspects.

Aspects may also come from unresolved relationship corridors with other people. In the first meditation in Part One, the light was focused on the solar plexus to dissolve any tentacles from one's stomach area. These tentacles connect into one's solar plexus from outside one's energy field. Quite often, these tentacles are attached to another person and form through unresolved issues between one and others - primarily family members, lovers and spouses. Once one heals these aspects, and brings them home, one harmonises one's energy field. One's vibrational frequency then ascends into a higher level and this makes it easier to receive higher levels of information through the channelling system. Clearing aspects is very important because unresolved anger, fear, jealousy, prejudices and judgments will make it difficult for one to channel the higher vibrational frequencies of fifth dimensional beings.

It is very important for a channel to work consciously on clearing his or her lower aspects. It is just as important for the channel to remain clear of these lower aspects or to resolve them as they arise, as it is to bring forth the channelling itself. Often people are concerned about protection when channelling. They are worried that lower spirits may enter into the energy field and take over. A channel's best protection is to keep her energy field clear. Even the most experienced channels - people who have channelled for many years to many clients – will, at certain times, need to do their own inner work to resolve their lower aspects. Experienced channels make this commitment because they are well aware that if they do not ascend and move forward into higher levels of their own spiritual pathway, it is very difficult to facilitate this level of moving forward or ascension in others. By keeping one's energy field clear, one may relax knowing that the messages one brings forth are of the highest integrity.

The Aspect Therapy Meditation at the end of this chapter is designed to assist in two ways: as a further exploration of one's aspects and as a meditation to heal lower aspects.

Another way to clear unresolved aspects is through counselling. Some people find the process of talking allows them to bring up unresolved issues and is sufficient to clear the problem and help release the aspect. Kinesiology is another very powerful way to clear unresolved aspects because kinesiology has the ability to identify the aspect specifically, understand why it exists, release it from the body cell memory and then test whether the aspect has released on all levels. The aspect will not clear until the initiate has identified and accepted sufficient feelings or beliefs belonging to the aspect. This is often why, with intense clearing, people feel that the same issue keeps presenting itself or the same feelings keep coming around. These cycles continue until one connects into the very core of those feelings or the very core reason for the aspect's existence. Once one understands the core reasons for the aspect's existence, the aspect truly transcends and returns home.

Unresolved aspects can sometimes be like naughty children in one's energy field that do all sorts of unhelpful and annoying things to get one's attention. When an aspect is being ignored, it often resorts to creating chaos in one's life, causing events such as traumas and accidents. When one inadvertently creates something that one wishes one hadn't, this is often an aspect trying to get attention. Use the Aspect Therapy Meditation below, or other helpful techniques, to understand what the aspect is trying to communicate. Likewise with certain addictions, sometimes an addiction is associated with a particular aspect or cluster of aspects. As one systematically works through this cluster of aspects, one understands the aspects and allows the aspects to express themselves in safe ways. In such situations, as in all cases of behavioural concern or disruption, it might be advisable to seek the assistance of a trusted and qualified practitioner.

Occasionally, an aspect may manifest as something different from what it is. With melancholia for example, one may call forth the aspect that is feeling melancholic, communicate with it and clear that aspect, but the feeling returns hours or days later. Explore underneath the melancholic aspect. The aspect may be melancholic on the surface, but be angry or fearful deep down. With Aspect Therapy or through other forms of therapy, it is very important to always seek the very core of the aspects. When gardening, weeds do not clear away permanently unless the roots are removed. It is exactly the same with aspects. If an initiate flits across the surface or deals with things on the superficial level by asking too many people for advice or consulting too many healers rather than sitting down with herself and engaging in honest self-enquiry about a particular issue, the issue will keep returning.

Channels who take time to engage in thorough self-examination are then able to gain access to higher vibrational frequencies and facilitate more effective healing, educational and channelling sessions for other people. This does not mean that one must be '100% clear and perfect' in every session that one facilitates. No one is perfect. There are some people on the planet who are enlightened, but for most, it is a gradual process of unfolding. However, it is important to resolve pressing issues before channelling for others as this ensures one reaches a higher level of information and connects with one's true Gateway Guardian to assist with the session.

As one starts clearing aspects, a signal releases in the energy field to all unresolved aspects indicating that work has truly begun. It is as though an invitation to come home is issued to all one's aspects. When an initiate starts Aspect Therapy or other forms of intense clearing, it is as if 'Pandora's Box' opens and every aspect that has ever felt unresolved will present and want to be cleared. This process is intense and can feel as though it goes on forever and there is no end to it. Perhaps there is no end to it until one reaches enlightenment. However, the intensity of clearing aspects will lessen over time. As tiring and at times overwhelming as it can be, it is important to keep clearing the aspects. If the initiate leaves tender or raw aspects for too long in the energy field they become stuck, heavy and very uncomfortable. One must keep clearing them even if this feels as though one is in meditation four times a day. The intensity of the clearing will eventually subside.

If aspects are left stuck in the energy field, it is not only uncomfortable for the initiate, it is uncomfortable for friends and family who have to live with the aspect's behaviours and emotions. If an aspect is very difficult to transmute, call in some help from trustworthy people who are capable of aiding at that higher level. Traditional healing disciplines, exercise based on ancient techniques, and homeopathy may relieve tension in the body, blockages in the emotional body, and help to release the aspect.

Walking in nature has a profound ability to shift blockages. Gardening helps distract the mind from worrying about the aspect, and after a little while in the garden, the energy seems to clear. One is still likely to need to return to meditation and communicate with the aspect to ensure it is on its way to being healed. Nature makes it easier to receive a clear channel when one enters into meditation again. This is simply because nature helps anchor energy. Sometimes, when working to clear aspects, the energy can become quite congested in the head, clogging the mind, and leaving it quite confused or with heavy thoughts and thinking processes. It is important to anchor the mind's energy by spending time with nature. This grounds the energy and makes it much easier to settle when one returns to meditation. This involves Mother Nature in the healing process and allows the nature beings to facilitate a deeper level of healing. Nature is a most powerful spiritual healer, soothing unresolved aspects until they are ready to let go of their pain and heal completely.

Normally functioning aspects become unresolved aspects when they were not able to process certain emotions and experiences at the time they occurred. For example, a part of oneself may come forward in meditation as an unresolved aspect who presents as a small child. This part talks about how it feels or about its pain and specific situations. When it communicates these experiences, it begins to release what happened and finally set itself free so that it can return home to love and move upwardly. For aspects such as these where a childhood part is involved, nature can be particularly soothing. Thus, meditating outside in a garden or in the sunshine often assists to help the aspect feel safe and comfortable.

One's unresolved aspects are not one's enemies. They are parts of oneself that need love and healing and who, in most cases, are desperate to come home. They are parts that must feel safe enough to come home and they will generally feel safe enough through the gentle process of Aspect Therapy. Again, meditating in a safe, warm environment in nature or surrounded by natural things, will assist the aspect to feel supported.

Occasionally some aspects come forward from a past life. They may be dressed differently or will appear differently, according to the customs and beliefs they held at the time. People with spiritual etheric sight, may even see a vision of their aspect's lifetime, like watching a scene on a movie screen.

This may provide a greater understanding of these aspects so that one may develop greater compassion for them.

Though this happens rarely, an aspect from a past life may come forward and try to present itself as a guide. It is important that one does not confuse these aspects with guides. One does not want to channel an aspect who is unresolved as a guide or as a guiding light for another person. One must call forth one's Gateway Guardian to clarify the status of the being who presents, to ensure one channels beings who are of the higher vibrational frequency of the fifth dimensional level and above. Exceptions to this are, of course, if one is on a specific assignment as a medium where one's extensive training allows one to channel third and fourth dimensional beings. Generally, one does not want to channel unresolved aspects of oneself from past lives. Aspect Therapy is designed to address these aspects through allowing them to heal and ascend. Once they have ascended they may then return in the future as guides and/or to offer assistance.

Sometimes in Aspect Therapy Meditation, lower spirits may present, masquerading as one's own aspects. One must not seek to resolve these lower spirits or bring them home into one's energy field. These lower spirits are easily identifiable because they may 'jump around' in meditation. Receiving a clear vision of these aspects or clear answers is very difficult. Usually lower spirits will not communicate or if they do talk, the communication is not clear, it is not forthcoming and the answers are confusing or contradictory. Do not entertain these lower spirits and instead call forth Archangel Michael and allow him to shine light on them. This light will transmute anything that does not serve one's highest benefit and will clear away the lower entities. Whatever remains needs to be processed as unresolved aspects.

Aspects are processed by first allowing them to say everything they need to say in order to release them of the burden they have carried for years or lifetimes. Once the aspect has communicated all that it needs to, and it is satisfied that its plight is genuinely understood, the aspect can then be resolved by placing it either in a cylinder of violet light or transmuting it into the light. The aspect is essentially lifted up into the fifth dimension, or if an aspect is an inner child or part of one's physical identity in this life, this part will merge back into one's physical body, usually entering through the heart centre. The aspect will naturally choose what it needs to do.

In some cases, the aspect will remain where it stands and it will not return or transmute. Generally, the aspect refuses to return because one has not seen the core reason that it presented in the first place. One has not looked at the core reason or explanation for the aspect's existence. Resume dialogue with this aspect and ask for the core reason for its pain. Do not guess or pre-empt what the aspect wants to say. Listen to what it needs to say as quite often the aspect is unresolved because no one has listened to it. It is important that one does not repeat that pattern. The aspect needs attention, it needs to be heard, and it needs unconditional love and acceptance, and an invitation to return home.

Aspect Therapy Meditation

Sit quietly and relax.

Visualise a place of safety

Sit quietly in this place of safety.

Feel or see the presence of Archangel Michael. Feel the loving support of this being of light.

Look into the distance and sense or see a being coming forward. This being is an unresolved aspect of you in need of healing and ready to be set free.

Sense whether this aspect is male or female, how old this aspect is, and try to sense what this aspect is feeling.

This aspect will now stand a few metres away, next to Archangel Michael. Archangel Michael will shine light on this aspect. This will make it easier to see the aspect clearly. Archangel Michael's light clears away any confusion.

Ask the aspect: "Why have you come today? What do you need me to see in order for you to be set free today?"

Listen closely to the aspect's answer. Ask the aspect to talk about all the things it needs to say, all the things it must express in order for it to be released.

If the aspect has trouble communicating, ask Archangel Michael to shine extra light on the aspect. This light will serve to nurture the aspect and help it feel safe. If the aspect struggles to communicate about deeper feelings or fears, start with simple questions like: "How old are you?"

When the aspect communicates freely, explore it further by asking: "What is your core pain?" And then: "Have I understood all that I need to in order for you to be set free today?" Wait patiently for the aspect to respond.

When the aspect is ready to be healed, allow the aspect to experience the full might and healing of Archangel Michael. The light will flow through the aspect and it may transform immediately - it may grow, it may change, it may fill with light.

Alternatively, the aspect may want to return to your physical body. It may merge into your heart centre or it may wish to go home to the higher realms.

If it wishes to go home to the higher realms, visualise a cylinder of powerful vibrant violet light. This cylinder of violet light stands in the corner of your place of safety.

Ask the aspect: "Are you ready to go into the cylinder of violet light now?" It will choose whether to go into the cylinder of violet light to be lifted up into the higher realms, home to the fifth dimension. The cylinder will travel higher and higher until it disappears from view.

If the aspect chooses to merge with your physical body, feel the energy of the aspect merging into your heart centre, ceasing the separation and returning home to oneness.

Archangel Michael stands nearby. Call forth any other aspects that need to be healed this day. If more than one aspect presents, do not be concerned about this. Sometimes aspects come in clusters and they are connected by a similar theme. Ask to understand the core issues that connect these aspects. Ask the aspects to communicate about what they need to in order to be set free.

Once the aspect or aspects have completed saying all that they need to in order to set themselves free, ask them to choose their path of healing. They will now either merge with your heart or return home in the cylinder of violet light.

Return to your awareness of your place of safety and Archangel Michael. Ask Archangel Michael to send healing energy and light through your energy field to strengthen it and fill it with energy, light and love. After this process of intense healing, take a deep breath in and gently return from meditation.

Sometimes, during Aspect Therapy Meditation, people fall asleep. Generally, this is because an aspect has surfaced that holds certain emotions that one finds confronting. It can be quite difficult to stay present through this type of intense clearing. If one continues to fall asleep, even after several meditation sessions, it is important not to dismiss this. Take some time in nature to anchor the energies or perhaps try a different time of day to meditate. Some people find meditating late at night is difficult because they are already tired. Often people find meditating after lunch difficult because the body shuts down. If this is the case, set the alarm and wake up early to meditate when the energy is crisp and clear. This is usually between 4:00 a.m. and sunrise. This approach has its own rewards, especially if there is a stuck aspect inhibiting one's progress. If one still finds it is difficult to clear an aspect, rest, go outside and do something enjoyable and positive before returning to meditation.

Universal Core Aspects

Occasionally an initiate knows intuitively that she has an aspect in need of clearing and yet her mind will not focus enough to allow the aspect to come forward in meditation. In this instance, it is useful to focus on a Universal Core Aspect. A universal core aspect is present in most human incarnated light-workers who have not previously cleared the aspect in this life or other lifetimes. Its reason for existing will vary from person to person, and it will exist because of events that occurred in this lifetime and previous incarnations. Outlined below are the descriptions of the three main universal core aspects. Use the Aspect Therapy Meditation to heal these aspects.

First Core Aspect: Self-doubt

The first core aspect keeps the seeds of self-doubt alive within one's mind. It feels unworthy in the light of the Divine Presence. The first core aspect believes it or its hierarchy is unworthy or inadequate for some reason. In meditation, call forth this aspect, asking it to present itself for healing. Talk to it about why it feels unworthy or inadequate.

Second Core Aspect: Fear of abandonment

The second core aspect holds a deep fear that the higher realms will abandon or reject it. This aspect may also feel abandoned by the higher realms or hold a belief that the higher realms abandoned it during a past life or at some stage in its history.

Second Core Aspect: Fear of abandonment sub-aspect level one

This sub-aspect of the second core aspect holds anger or rage towards the higher realms because of its belief that the higher realms abandoned it. If an initiate suspects that it has this sub-aspect in its hierarchy, it is essential to heal it before beginning work as a channel for others. This level of anger can taint the quality of a channel's work and draw lower vibrational entities to one's channelling system. Send violet light through the solar plexus initially to transmute any anger. The solar plexus chakra is clear when the violet light's work completes and the golden light begins to flow freely through the centre.

Second Core Aspect: Fear of abandonment sub-aspect level two

To access and heal this second sub-aspect, enter meditation to locate a time in one's life/past life where an aspect of oneself turned away from the highest path, or inner knowing. The aspect may also believe that it abandoned the higher realms or the noble highest path. Heal the aspect through the Aspect Therapy Meditation or another preferred technique.

Third Core Aspect – The Third Dimensional Survival Self

The third core aspect is particularly relevant to those who have incarnated many times. It is an aspect that focuses on what it believes it needs to do to help its human body to survive in the physical world. It is a third dimensional aspect. It holds the energy for the survival frequency. It is the aspect that coaxes and coaches the other aspects to survive the physical life. It can appear as a protective guard, or as a manipulative, calculating, or scheming aspect. It will have adopted certain character traits and survival techniques. It will have particular ways of operating to ensure its survival in the third dimension. As one clears this central aspect that is attached to the third dimension, other sub-aspects that contain coping mechanisms, behaviours and strategies will arise. These sub-aspects and their strategies are no longer needed once the higher self becomes the leader of the human initiate in the physical world. The higher self has a toolbox of its own such as intuition, wisdom and knowingness – and moreover, an abiding faith that the essence of Soul is eternal.

Encouraging this central third dimensional aspect to surrender control to one's higher self can be a multi-layered task – a task not usually achieved in one or two meditations. The central third dimensional aspect is clever, well established in its role, and has plenty of precautions in place to ensure it is not displaced. Remember, its core reason for existing is to ensure that one's human self survives the third dimensional life on Earth. It has employed every strategy and belief system necessary to ensure its safety and survival. A wily performer, it has gathered its particular form of intelligence from its early childhood environment, such as family, friends, school and social influences through community and media. Gradually over many meditations, this third dimensional aspect will dissolve or ascend and allow one's higher self to take command and suffuse the initiate with its own belief in the everlasting nature of the soul.

PART FOUR

Channelling Ethics and Channelling for Others

Channelling is a natural by-product of wanting to be useful to others and consciously connecting with the Spiritual Hierarchy for Earth, the grand light structure that houses the hierarchies of human incarnates and oversees the Earth assignment. Once one is consciously connected, it follows that one volunteers, or is asked by one's hierarchy, to aid others to reconnect also. There are occasions where by interacting with the Spiritual Hierarchy for Earth on behalf of fellow initiates, one can utilise one's connection to help others to form their own connection. It is at this time that one becomes a channel for others.

By completing the exercises in the book thus far, one has begun to familiarise oneself with a clear formula on how to safely and easily open the channelling system. Although initially it may not appear that things are transforming, one is awakening communication with higher councils and beings of light who live within the vast realms and dimensions overlapping with Earth's physical plane. This transformation is occurring on the subtle levels of one's energy field, within one's consciousness and in the deepest part of one's chakras. Soon, one will develop the confidence to trust wholly in the messages one receives through one's channelling system, and, where appropriate, share these messages with others.

Once the channelling system is established, ongoing commitment is required to keep it active. The following pages offer further suggestions and exercises to strengthen one's role as a channel for oneself and others, working for one's hierarchy and/or the Spiritual Hierarchy for Earth, and understanding the code of ethics that accompanies working in this way.

Code of Ethics

The code of ethics for channels is an unwritten one. There is no earthly board or committee to which one must answer. The code of ethics adheres to basic universal law. Channels who understand the law and work in harmony with it, find the channelling path very rewarding. One feels good about one's work, one's abilities increase over time rather than diminish, and one's own sense of wellbeing increases, as the channelling path becomes a way to know oneself as well as to aid others. Working in harmony with the universal law increases one's protection from any unhelpful energetic influences, such as entities, spirits that have not made their transition through to the higher planes, and the emotional challenges of one's clients.

The code of ethics divides into two sections that work hand in hand: the universal law, and channelling principles. The universal law is an integral part within the workings of the All That Is and every interaction on Earth's floor. It cannot be separate from the All That Is, and is permanent and unchanging. It is the formula that allows the All That Is to function harmoniously. Channelling principles are specific to channelling.

The key aspect of universal law is the Law of One: *When all are allowed to be within their frequencies, all shall come into peace and harmony.* This law is relevant to the channel when working with clients and their choices. The channel may suggest a beneficial course of action to the client, even express an opinion if asked, but the channel enters unwise territory if she/he projects her will onto the client. A desire to see one's will obeyed by the client will at best bring confusion and disharmony into the client's session. At worst, this behaviour can push a client to make a choice because she feels fearful or intimidated. A choice made from this space will set a fear-based cycle in motion that the client will need to resolve down the track.

Channels who use their channelling to gain control over others by having their will obeyed attract spirits/entities of a lower vibrational frequency. A channel who intends to control others and abuse her power will attract spirits to channel that are abusive in various ways. Channels, who hold the higher intention in their minds and hearts to be of service in a way that serves the highest good and will of all, attract higher beings of light, also of that intention.

The universal law encourages a state of acceptance, allowing others to be as they are without judgment or the belief that one must rescue, change, subjugate or enslave others. This unspoken understanding that the client can clear, shift or change at her own pace and only when she is ready to, immediately puts the clients at ease.

Though it is important to remember that becoming a channel is not conditional on finding a teacher, some aspirants choose that path. A spiritual teacher may insist upon certain behaviour or a code being adhered to before accepting a student, or continuing their study. This is appropriate providing the teacher is aligned to the Law of One and/or a tradition that is aligned to the Law of One. A channel who takes on students may refuse to train a particular student unless the student modifies his/her behaviour. This too is appropriate if the student's behaviour is not conducive to the higher lessons taught in the class. This expectation upon the student to change is not against the Law of One and is necessary at certain stages in a student's learning. The core intention behind the teacher's request that the student changes his/her behaviour is the determining factor in whether the teacher is acting in integrity and in alignment to the Law of One. There are instances where matters between teachers and students, channels and clients are brought before the High Council of the Law of One. Always, it is the intention behind the behaviour that is identified as key to the situation.

Channelling for Other People

Some channels prefer to keep their ability to channel to themselves, or share it only with their immediate family and closest friends. Others choose to work as professional channels or bring channelling into their existing work as a practitioner in the health or healing industry.

The ability to communicate with the higher realms is a wonderful gift to share with people. However, choosing to channel for other people raises important issues. People have different opinions about the channel's role in modern society. It is essential, if one chooses to channel for others, to explore these opinions to gain an understanding of what people may expect from a channelling session. One must explore one's own thoughts about a channel's role, and consider the ethical issues that accompany all professions that place the practitioner in a position of power. A channel, by definition, is often automatically placed in a position of power in clients' eyes. Simply because of the channel's ability to converse with the higher realms, she has the potential to influence the choices that clients make, which in turn, alters the framework of their lives. A channel must first acknowledge this potential power in order to work responsibly with clients.

Reflecting on these elements early in one's career assists in determining what type of role one will provide, therefore what a client can expect from a consultation, and what is better handled by another type of practitioner. This is the first step to establishing the boundaries one will require in order to operate a safe, professional practice as a channel. For example, a channel may wish to stipulate that he does not offer any advice on a client's medications, he does not diagnose any illnesses and does not advise on medical decisions regarding the treatment of disease. He may ask his clients to seek the assistance of medical practitioners specialising in either traditional or modern medicine. His work may, however, encourage a client to talk about their lives or aspects of themselves that may be inextricably linked with their general state of being and explore ways to bring harmony into their lives, which might in turn have a positive impact on their overall level of health.

Learning to respond appropriately to challenging questions is a vital part of enjoying one's practice as a channel. People ask channels to search for answers to all manner of queries. If one is uncertain about whether to answer a particular question, one should enter meditation and ask one's Gateway Guardian. Always, it is important to refer to one's guardian and one's own intuition, if one is feeling pressured by other people.

Sometimes a person will visit a channel because he is in a situation where he feels quite desperate for answers. This desperation must not be allowed to create pressure to the point where one finds it difficult to see one's role professionally. A channel is responsible for the clarity of the channelling system, for the cleanliness of her energy field, and for ensuring that she communicates with beings of the fifth dimension and beyond (unless she is a medium and communicates with the spirits of people who have left their physical bodies behind, but have not yet reached the fifth dimension). A channel is not responsible for answers received that may not please or satisfy the person receiving the channelling. A channel is not responsible to find the answer to questions that she does not have permission to answer, such as questions about other people's private affairs.

Clients regularly ask questions about their spouses, other family members, their boyfriend or girlfriend, business partners or business people in opposition to them. Sometimes it may be a very fine line which separates the questions that which spring from a desire to seek the higher path from those which serve a lesser intention. It is important in these situations that the channel communicates with her Gateway Guardian and asks her Gateway Guardian: "Do I have permission to work with this person on these issues?" As one develops a strong relationship with one's Gateway Guardian, one learns to sense very clearly "yes" answers from "no" answers.

The clarity of yes/no questioning develops over time. Questions such as: "What do I need to do to move forward?" or "What can help me open my channels?" are broad questions, allowing the answer to be open and not specific or narrowed down to a simple "yes" or "no." These are useful questions with which to practise. In this regard, the exercise at the end of this part provides futher guidance. With time it becomes easier to recognise or sense the difference between "yes" and "no" answers. The channel will reach the stage where she is able to ask her Gateway Guardian: "Do I have permission to conduct this session with this person and answer questions about other people?" and feel very clearly whether the answer is "yes" or "no."

Other times a client may put the channel on the spot, particularly halfway through a consultation, making it difficult for the channel to take the time to ask her Gateway Guardian if it is wise to proceed. In this instance, it is important to trust one's instinct. If something does not feel right do not proceed with the channelling, however cancel the session in a way that does not leave the client feeling blamed or unworthy. It is better to choose this course of action rather than conduct a session that does not feel right. Channels who do not establish strategies to deal with uncomfortable situations that may arise in a consultation often have quite short careers where they feel vulnerable and need breaks from the role.

Write down a policy regarding the circumstances and conditions that one requires before conducting a channelling session. One example of a policy may be to seek the permission of parents before channelling to a client under the age of 18 years, consistent with what is generally recognised as the age of independence in the wider community. Although some teenagers experience transformational results in the way they view their lives after receiving a channelling, some parents do not feel comfortable about allowing channels to work with their children. Some parents may need to sit in on their child's session and the channel may need to allow this in order to secure permission to communicate a channelled message to a child.

In the case of people who suffer certain forms of mental illness, it may not be in their best interest to receive a channelling. Sometimes, this type of client may find the messages confusing, which may add to their suffering. In such cases, follow the Gateway Guardian's counsel. Occasionally a client who has suffered mental illness, but is recovering, and who is under the care of a psychologist or psychiatrist, may approach a channel for a session. In this situation, ask the client to communicate with her clinician about her interest in having a channelling session and also follow up by telephoning the therapist to discuss the basic outline of what will happen in a session. This should only be done with the consent of the client. The psychiatrist and the channel should be able to discuss whether the session is likely to benefit the client or destabilise her, depending on the nature of the illness and stage of recovery.

Some practitioners in the healing or channelling field feel intimidated by members of the medical profession, particularly psychiatrists, believing them to be hostile to 'alternative treatments'. It is important to explore one's own feelings and prejudices towards psychiatrists or other such specialists to be better equipped to create bridges with them if one's work requires one to do so. If afraid of being judged by a psychiatrist for conducting an unprofessional or unethical practice, investigate this fear. Some channels carry old fears that they might be secretly 'crazy' or 'mad', because of their ability to hear the 'otherworld'. Acknowledge any aspects that carry these fears in order to work confidently as a channel. Some channels go through periods of feeling inauthentic, as if they are somehow engaged in a sham or a masquerade. Work through these areas with a trusted mentor, perhaps even a psychiatrist, until the issues are resolved. This personal groundwork will help one to liaise comfortably with medical practitioners if or when one's practice requires it.

Many psychiatrists are indeed sympathetic to the need in some clients to explore their spiritual life as part of their healing process. Prominent Swiss psychiatrist Carl Jung (1875-1961) assisted in opening this door through his documented journeys into the unconscious and his interaction with Philemon, a being who came to him through a vision, and was for him, for a period in his life, what some might call a guru[1]. In his book, *Memories, Dreams and Reflections,* Carl Jung writes about a discussion he has with one of Gandhi's friends, someone he considers highly cultivated. The elderly gentleman explains to Jung that there are ghostly gurus as well as human ones, and although most people have human gurus, some have spirit teachers. For Jung, this information was illuminating and reassuring for it gave him a different context in which to view his association with Philemon. Thus he writes: "Evidently, then, I had not plummeted right out of the human world, but had only experienced the sort of thing that could happen to others who made similar efforts."[2]

The overlapping of the higher realms into the manifested world is stronger for some than others. For those who cannot deny their relationship with the 'otherworld' and its presence in their lives, a spiritual approach is a necessary component, if not the central component, of their healing from mental illness. Again, Jung describes a case study of a young Jewish woman suffering from severe anxiety neurosis whose primary focus was centred on her physical appearance and flirtatious activity. Jung received the key to her treatment through his dreams, and an approach to treating her was thus devised: "I had to awaken mythological and religious ideas in her, for she belonged to that class of human beings of whom spiritual activity is demanded. Thus her life took on a meaning, and no trace of the neurosis was left."[3]

Jung recognised that individuals required the opportunity and the freedom to gaze upon the spiritual horizon and allow its presence to interact with the spiritual self within them. This contact with the spiritual dimension brought tremendous healing to the spiritual self that had been rejected and starved. Without this, life becomes too narrow and restrictive for particular patients, and the spiritual element they lacked was generally sought by the

1 C.G Jung: *Memories, Dreams and Reflections,* Random House Vintage Books Edition, New York 1989, p.183

2 C.G Jung: *Memories, Dreams and Reflections,* Random House Vintage Books Edition, New York 1989, p.184

3 C.G Jung: *Memories, Dreams and Reflections,* Random House Vintage Books Edition, New York 1989, p.139

personality through outward successes or presented by the unconscious in ways that disturbed the patient. As in the case above, through helping his patient recognise the need for the spiritual element in her life, the neurosis vanished. As a representative of many clients then and today, she needed a pathway out of her superficial life and into a life that held greater meaning.

These and other observations led Jung to stress the importance of the spiritual dimension and the central role of Soul on the path to healing. As one psychologist and author in the field has noted, Jung would "return a patient to (their) his ancestral religion as quickly as possible" [4], wherever feasible. While he recognised that might not always be possible, what can be discerned from this approach was the value Jung ascribed to belief in some form of the Divine – however that might be perceived, or some attachment to spiritual principles, for the healthy functioning of the human psyche. (A significant influence at the time, his thinking continues today to resonate deeply with those seeking a more wholistic perspective on the human condition.)

A therapist who may not be equipped to provide the keys to that pathway, perhaps through lack of exploration of it in himself, may have the insight to recognise the benefits they offer for his patient and that they may need to be sought outside his own treatment. This is where a healer or channel may have a role to play, possibly facilitating the opening of that pathway in the patient. When the higher realms reach down through a channel and make contact with a patient who yearns to reconnect with the spiritual nature of life, profound healing can occur quite quickly. In this way, the channel becomes a healer. The energy that flows through the channel soothes and reassures the client, and the words that flow through bring the client greater understanding of her life path and the challenges she faces.

Some psychologists and psychiatrists are understandably concerned about predictive channelling that may give false hope to a client or encourage the client to take a path that he/she may not have given due consideration. For a patient who is particularly vulnerable, a predictive channelling that does not 'come true' may contribute to a patient feeling like he/she has failed or was abandoned by the higher realms. There are several reasons why a predictive channelling may not 'come true'. The channel may have allowed the projected desires of the client to impress upon his/her channels, clouding the clarity of

---

4 Robert A. Johnson: *The Psychology of Romantic Love*, Arkana, England 1987, p.186

the message. The channel may be unclear, channelling a lower entity rather than a fifth dimensional being. The client may have unconsciously or consciously chosen a path different to the one predicted, as is her freewill right.

If the prediction accompanies some inner work the client needs to do, such as the clearing away of an unresolved aspect of herself, usually the prediction will not manifest unless the inner work is done to allow this higher unfolding of the prediction. Fifth dimensional beings generally describe the highest potential of what is possible for the client, and show the client what fears and limitations to address and clear away so that this highest potential is realised. A channel simply cannot be responsible for a channelling not 'coming true' if the client desires the highest potential predicted for him/her without undertaking the necessary steps of self-healing to allow the highest path to manifest.

Because of this, a client really needs to be able to identify that she is in control of her thoughts and her choices, and is ultimately responsible for how her path manifests, in order for a channelling session to be useful. It is important to liaise with the therapist treating the patient to determine how vulnerable the patient is prior to the channelling session. For a normally functioning person, channelling - with or without a predictive element - can open up other doorways of possibility; open the client's mind to higher thoughts and encourage the client to pursue a potentially higher path that he/she hadn't considered before. In this way, predictive channelling can inspire and motivate others. Creative people often use channelling sessions to stimulate the formation of new ideas in their minds.

To reiterate, just as it is not advisable to channel to people who are presently unable to take responsibility for the way their lives manifest, so also one may find it necessary to reconsider channelling to a client who is very attached to an outcome. People who are very attached to a particular outcome can be difficult clients because they may unconsciously project their thoughts onto the channel's channelling system causing confusion in the answers that the channel receives or making it difficult to secure clear messages. This arises when people are very attached to receiving unequivocal "yes" and "no" answers; a scenario which often arises with questions like "Will I get that job?" or "Will this relationship work out?" or "Will this person propose to me?".

These types of questions are often better left in the hands of a psychic. A psychic looks into the area around her client. She reads his intention, and his choices that have not yet manifested. The psychic may also be able to detect people attached to her client and read their intentions and their choices that are yet to manifest. With this information, the psychic is able to predict the most likely outcome, providing the client and people associated with the client, do not make radical changes in the near future, which would change what is likely to manifest. A channel on the other hand, accesses her Gateway Guardian or other beings and asks for information about her client's situation. She does not engage her psychic gifts to add to the information her Gateway Guardian supplies. She does not offer an interpretation of the channelled message and does not offer a prediction based on anything she sees or senses.

Many people in need of clear answers to specific questions prefer to go to a psychic to increase their chances of having their questions answered directly, as psychics may have greater scope to work this way and unlike channels, are not bound by 'rules' that restrict offering one's interpretation. Channels rarely combine psychic reading and channelling to obtain answers in their professional consultations, mainly because many Gateway Guardians and guides prefer their messages to be received in their pure form without the channel's limited or potentially biased interpretation. Psychics generally have freer reign to interpret psychically obtained information because the client and the psychic have an understanding that the interpretation of signs, cards or other divination tools is an integral component of the psychic reading session. When a person goes to a channel, it is often because she does not want a human's interpretation and wants only information from the higher realms, regardless of whether it addresses her questions directly.

If a channel feels that it is her role to address questions that may be better put to a psychic, it is important that the boundary - the energy around one's emotional, mental and etheric bodies - is clear enough so that she is not unconsciously influenced by what the client wants to hear rather than what the higher message truly is. One must train oneself to listen to one's own counsel. In many ways, this is the key to channelling. By staying true to one's integrity and higher instructions, regardless of the projections or desires of others, one will be ultimately respected by others as a clear, authentic channel.

When the Channelling System Is Not Working

Over the course of a long career, some channels experience short 'shut down' phases, quiet times when their channelling ability feels weak or even non-existent. There are various reasons why the channelling system may be blocked. Sometimes channelling systems close temporarily because the person is physically exhausted. Under extreme tiredness, channelling systems do not operate as well as they should. Usually beings of light such as Gateway Guardians will rest the channelling system until the physical body has entered into a new phase of healing or rejuvenation. If a person has been very unwell or is physically exhausted, often a Gateway Guardian or the person's higher self will temporarily close the channelling system down. Although channelling can contribute vast amounts of energy to an individual channel, it can also use the person's energy to transmit a message. A person's Gateway Guardian will not exhaust the physical body for the sake of receiving channelling. After the body heals and is strong enough, the channels will naturally reawaken.

When in the midst of intense personal development or clearing where unresolved aspects are coming to the surface of one's awareness, one's higher self and Gateway Guardian may close the channelling system down. This is for a channel's protection as well as the protection of other people who come for healing or channelling. If one is transmuting clusters of lower aspects and the lower emotional states that accompany the aspects, one's frequency bands are very much in the third or fourth dimension. This leaves the channelling system more susceptible to accidently attracting a lower entity or a lower spirit trying to pass itself off as a higher vibrational being. When one's higher self and Gateway Guardian close the channelling system down for safety, they will open it up again as soon as the unresolved aspects clear. This policy is in no way a test or a punishment for having unresolved aspects; it is simply a safeguard.

Then, as one ascends into higher vibrational frequencies, one's channelling system adjusts accordingly. After a period of consolidation, it will then again be time for acceleration. One connects to a higher channelling system after clearing enough to raise one's vibrational frequencies to allow compatibility with these higher levels.

Occasionally one's higher self or Gateway Guardian will deliberately close parts of the channelling system down to change it over. When taking out old shop fittings and putting the new fittings in, the shop cannot open for business while this change over is occurring. Channelling is very similar. One's channelling system will 'upgrade' as one heals unresolved aspects and moves upwardly into higher vibrational frequencies, making available more channels and higher channels or higher vibrational frequencies to flow through the channels. Through committing to one's own personal development and healing, one evolves as a channel and one's channelling system improves as a result, providing clearer messages.

When a channel's higher self and Gateway Guardian change over the channelling system, they may shut the channelling system down for weeks at a time. Although it can be a very confusing and uncomfortable time, generally one's higher self or Gateway Guardian gives notice in advance before it happens. When it is likely to occur, take a holiday or retreat or simply do something that avoids being too focused on channelling. Worrying about when communication will be re-established does not assist the process. The shutting down of the channelling system to connect the channel to higher vibrational frequencies is a natural, normal process that happens for all channels as they ascend and move up through the levels.

A very small number of channels on Earth have experienced the shutting down of their channelling systems due to their choice to abuse their power when channelling, misusing their channelling ability in order to gain power over others or manipulate others. If a channel undertakes negative or dark ritualistic work or spells designed to interfere with free will, the fifth dimension closes to the person's channelling system. If a channel wishes to operate a channelling system connected to fifth dimensional beings, the channel must align to the code that governs the fifth dimension. This code respects the right of all beings to exercise their free will right and does not seek to override this right by any means.

A person who chooses to channel to gain control of other people or manipulate in any way, will find it very difficult to maintain their access to higher channels. Fifth dimensional channels are only available to those who are aligned to the Law of One and Divine Will that flows through the fifth dimension. A channel can only access fifth dimensional information if his/her frequencies are compatible with that dimension. Compatibility is achieved when a channel's primary reason for channelling for others is to serve their highest good and will, to serve the Light, and to assist in some way to end the suffering of others by facilitating the anchoring of higher levels of understanding into humanity's consciousness.

It is important to set one's intention as a channel, possibly reaffirming this intention quietly before conducting a channelling session. Aligning to Divine Will ensures that the information that flows through is also aligned to Divine Will. Aligning to Divine Will allows one's fifth dimensional channelling system to open and expand and allows the channel to work for the Spiritual Hierarchy for Earth. As an incarnated, trusted channel for the Spiritual Hierarchy for Earth, one acts as a bridge of communication for others, holding that office for the rest of one's life if one desires it.

In the unlikely event that one abused the immense power that this position grants, the fifth dimensional capacity of one's channelling system would automatically close. In this rare case, the channel would be required to honour the codes of fifth dimensional channelling practice before the channelling system is reconnected to the vibrational frequencies held in the fifth dimension. This is a process that is monitored by the higher councils and is not, generally, facilitated by any physical teacher or aide incarnated on Earth. This prevents a channel from feeling that he/she is answerable to another human incarnate. Only the channel's higher council oversees the tests or requirements set for the channel to assist in reconnecting the channelling system with the fifth dimensional frequencies. The most direct path to allow reconnection is the surrendering of the aspect of oneself caught in fear and the belief that it must control or manipulate to stay protected, and the opening of the heart to trust and love.

Any person can turn to the Divine Source and return to the Light at any moment in order to work as a channel. One's integrity and desire to be of genuine service will be tested. These tests are not to be feared, but welcomed for they represent one's return to working with the fifth dimension. If one finds it difficult to feel safe during the process, one can meditate using Aspect Therapy, and call forth this aspect that feels afraid. Communicating with such aspects allows them to heal so that one can move forward and trust once more in the natural process of ascension.

Asking Questions and Receiving Direct Communication

Channelling is simply a type of communication between a human incarnate and the other realms. Initially it can appear more complicated and mysterious that what it actually is, but simply, it is a conversation, which will strengthen in its intensity the more often one communicates. Like all relationships, one's relationship with one's Gateway Guardian develops over time through the process of openness and communication. The channelling system develops automatically as one works with one's Gateway Guardian to understand and clear unresolved aspects. Through Aspect Therapy over the course of several weeks, one's own quiet meditation allows a form of channelling to occur.

At some point in a channel's development, the time may come to receive clear answers for other people. It is helpful to have a couple of willing people to 'practise on'. Choose people with whom one feels comfortable. It is useful to practise with at least two people in order to feel the difference in the energy when working with different people. In the following exercise keep a notebook and pen close by to write down messages or insights.

Asking Questions and Receiving Direct Communication Exercise

Sit in front of the channelling client.

Ask the client for her question. It is helpful in the beginning that the question doesn't require a definitive "yes" or "no" answer.

Write down the question. Once the question is clear, ask the person to close her eyes so that her staring at you is not a distraction.

Enter meditation and visualise a place of safety. Visualise Archangel Michael in the place of safety. You may see or sense one's Gateway Guardian standing in the place of safety. Because you are asking a question for another person, you may also sense another being close by. This is likely to be the client's higher self, Gateway Guardian or a guide.

Hold your client's question in your mind. Ask the Gateway Guardians and guides present for the answer to the person's question. Listen for the answer.

Either write down the answer in a notebook, try to remember it and speak it to the person or simply allow the words to flow through your voice, allowing your Gateway Guardian to speak directly.

It is beneficial to repeat this exercise above with other volunteers to feel the difference in the questions asked by different people, possibly sensing new guides and beings of light appearing for each person. At this stage, it is important to work directly with one's Gateway Guardian and even if other beings are present, ask those beings to stand in light of Archangel Michael to ensure that these beings are fifth dimensional. In this way the Gateway Guardian can be seen to function as a sort of filter or protector of the threshhold, admitting only other beings who are of the highest integrity and committed to the light.

Through working with questions from different people, one learns about one's Gateway Guardian and observes how the Gateway Guardian interacts with other beings of light. Sometimes one's Gateway Guardian will offer advice that may not make sense at the time. In these instances, it can be difficult to trust and follow this advice. Even though it may be confusing, often through following this guidance that doesn't make sense at the time, one finds that over time, the path becomes clear and one is pleased to have listened to this higher guidance and will be affirmed in following one's path as a channel. There is perhaps no greater service one can provide on Earth, for Earth and for others.

PART FIVE

In the Healing Room

The Routine

Every channel develops a 'routine' that helps them to prepare mentally and etherically before a client arrives. For some, an exercise such as the Energy Field Clearing Meditation may assist to strengthen their confidence and belief that they are prepared to channel. For others, a cup of tea and a walk around the garden may be all that is required to cleanse the mind of any 'noise' and help centre the mind for the session ahead. A channel sometimes receives channelled messages before the client arrives. Some messages may or may not be transmitted to the client, but at least have some value for the channel in preparing the session.

Before beginning the healing session, have all of the tools prepared in advance. Knowing that all the essential items are on hand produces a calming effect; thus a check-list (like the one below) is a good idea to ensure that everything will be ready – right down to a heatproof dish on which to lay any sage stick used in clearing.

Before channelling to a client, it is very useful to clear the client's energy field of external debris in a similar way to clearing one's own energy field as outlined in Part One.

Simple Healing Plan – Tools Needed and Suggested Process

Below is a basic healing plan with step-by-step instructions that guides the channel in how to conduct a healing session with the possibility of receiving messages for the client at the end of the session. As one becomes comfortable conducting healing sessions, one will expand naturally on the techniques suggested below.

Tools Needed

Healing/massage table for client to lie on and chair for healer to sit on

Pillow and warm blanket

Eye pillow or small face towel to cover client's eyes to help her relax

A cleansing/clearing oil such as lavender, eucalyptus, spearmint or lemongrass essential oil

Pen and paper or recording device if choosing to channel and record the messages

Glass of water and tissues for the client

Sage stick, heatproof dish for sage and matches to light it

Suggested Process

Take some time to mention details of the process to the client such as how long the session will take approximately, what she can expect, whether you will/won't tape the session etc. You may choose to take her questions now or let her ask questions progressively.

The client should be sitting upright on a comfortable chair or lying fully clothed on a healing/massage table with a blanket over the body for warmth as well as security. Quite often during a healing, the client's body temperature will drop substantially. If a client becomes too cold, she will become tense, agitated and possibly emotional. In hot weather, it may do to provide a light sheet so that the client still feels covered and not vulnerable or exposed.

Stand at the feet if the client is on a massage table or behind the body with hands on the shoulders if the client is on a chair. Some clients choose to sit, but most prefer to lie down and the exercise below is offered accordingly.

Ensure your client is comfortable lying down on the healing table.

Stand to the side of your client and consciously align your will to Divine Will. State in your mind that your intention is to serve the client's highest benefit. Place an amethyst crystal on her body. While this is not essential, it helps to signify the beginning of the session.

Following the Smudging exercise outlined in Part One, use sage to clear the outer layers of energy field. This clears any surface attachments and energetic debris. (Make sure burnt leaf does not fall on the person.)

When the sage clearing is complete, take a few minutes to visualise a violet cylinder at the client's feet.

Sit down on the chair and scan the client's energy field in your mind's eye, scanning for pockets of debris. Visualise debris transmuting.

Sprinkle a few drops of aromatherapy oil (eucalyptus or lavender) into your hands and run your hands through the layers of the client's energy field, as if brushing the energy field down. Sweep the debris down and away from the body into the violet light cylinder at the feet.

Stand up and move around the body as your intuition guides you. You may be drawn to a part of the body that needs more energy sent into it or lower energy lifted out of it. Go to that area and place your hands onto the area. If this area is near the chest of a woman or pelvic area of a man or a woman, do not rest your hands on the body, but hover your hands a foot above the body so that your actions do not invade your client's private space.

If you locate a pocket of debris or dark spot that is difficult to transmute, call on Archangel Michael to assist.

Now stand at the crown and scan the entire energy field. Are there any murky deposits remaining? Send extra violet light through and transmute these. Once you are satisfied that the client's energy field is clear of etheric debris, sit in your chair and begin receiving chan-nelled messages for the client. You may receive information only from your Gateway Guardian, or your guardian may usher in other beings to deliver messages, such as your client's Gateway Guardian, and other enlightened helpers such as archangels, saints and enlightened masters.

If you feel compelled at any stage to tone through your client's energy field or over a particular area of the body, allow the sounds to come gently at first so that you do not startle the client. (For further infor-mation about Toning, refer to the section below.)

When you sense the healing is complete, sit down in the seat, still your mind and enter meditation to ask your Gateway Guardian if there is anything else the higher councils would like you to do to help your client. Ask if there are any messages for the client. Speak the messages directly to the client or write them down.

In your mind thank the higher realms for allowing you to serve this client and then gently tell the client that the healing is complete.

You may wish to leave the room to allow your client a few minutes to herself to get up from the healing table in her own time. When you return to the room, offer her a glass of water. Be receptive to any ques-tions she may wish to raise with you at this point; allow her time to do so and to absorb the exchange.

Your client might like an explanation of certain messages. Consider refraining from explaining any channelled messages received so that the purity of the transmission is not affected by your interpretation. It is generally best for the client that she allows the healing to integrate and the messages to reveal their deeper meaning over time.

Incorporating Toning into the Channelling/Healing Session

One's voice has the ability to be a powerful healing tool. Toning is the process of entering the stillness within and accessing the tone or sound that is present within the body or a sound drawn from another realm or higher plane. Toning is an effective tool used by channels and healers. When using toning as part of a channelling session, the channel enters the still place within him and locates the sound building inside his body. When he opens his mouth to tone, the sound moves through his heart, into his throat and up through his crown chakra. The tone then enters the space between the crown and the Higher Self and Incarnation Team filling the channelling system bridge with its powerful vibrational frequency.

Toning itself may fulfil several functions:

It is able to release a vibration through the space to clear lower energy or disturbance.

It reinforces the outer boundary of the channelling system with its vibrational frequency, ensuring that lower energy and even the thoughts of the client cannot penetrate the space.

It further opens channels in the channelling system, sending a signal that it is time to work, and it also calls to higher beings to assist.

It centres the channel, releasing his tension and prepares him energetically and mentally for work.

Toning can also be used as a healing tool to assist the client. When the healer tones, he releases the higher vibrational sound that he has called upon, sending it into the energy field of the client so that it may harmonise the existing energy in the client or lift lower energy out of the body, returning the energy to the fifth dimension. The lower energy may be an unresolved aspect of the client, a lower entity or spirit.

Before toning for the first time in a channelling/healing session, it is useful to practise toning so that one feels comfortable expressing sound in this way. People new to toning often worry about whether they can sing. Because toning is used to release blockages or clear lower energies, it does not always sound beautiful. Try not to be concerned about how it sounds. Focus instead on its effectiveness; emanating love from one's heart when toning is a powerful way of sending any lower energies to the fifth dimension.

The power of toning as a tool for healing and awakening comes as a gift and divine blessing from the Sea Realms. This is an ancient gift that was given to human incarnates by the representatives from the Sea Realms many thousands of years ago in the time that is commonly understood to be that of Atlantis. Since that time, many healers have held the keys to toning and have integrated the keys in ways that communities and societies have been comfortable accepting, such as spiritual and religious chants and even popular music.

In order for an initiate to connect to his most ancient toning knowledge and wisdom, before it was adapted to fit in with the socially accepted ideas about sound held in this life and previous lives, the initiate must reconnect to the Sea Realms, where the gift of toning originated. The meditation below assists one to remember one's ancient relationship with the Sea Realms and the communities of light that acts as guardians for the ancient keys of sound, specifically toning.

Meditation for Connecting to the Sea Realms

Close your eyes and relax your body.

Feel your spirit lift out of your body and lift into the sky.

Your spirit will automatically travel across land or sea to the centre of the land of Australia. You will see or sense desert stretched out before you.

Your spirit touches down on the firm earth below.

You look up and see a cave-like entrance nearby set into a large rock. You will sense, and possibly even see, an ancient guide of great power and wisdom waiting by the entrance.

Walk towards this guide. He will read your heart. When he feels it is appropriate, he will grant you permission to enter this sacred place and he will guide you into the cave.

You follow the path down into the cave, which dips deeper and deeper into the Earth.

You follow the path into a large room in the Earth where another ancient being waits for you. This being studies you closely, before beckoning you to follow him.

He takes you to a strange plasma wall in the cave and tells you to prepare to step through. He explains that you will step through into a very deep part of the ocean and even though you may not be able to see, someone will take your hand and be your guide. The moment this person holds your hand, you will be able to breathe underwater and your body temperature will alter to keep you warm.

You say goodbye and thank you to your guides, and step through the plasma wall into the sea.

Everything is dark. You feel a soft hand reaching out to take yours and you feel instantly assured. This being is Lady Neptune.

She guides you through the water. Ahead you see an oceanic kingdom lit by a white orb of light like an ethereal moon.

Lady Neptune leads you into the kingdom to a path.

You follow the path to a temple. You walk up the steps of the temple and enter through its large doors. Inside the temple is a Council of Light with beings sitting in a circle. There is a space kept for you and Lady Neptune in the circle, and you take your seat.

The council explains to you that there is an aspect of yourself that they want you to meet. This is your 'oceanic self', the aspect of you and your hierarchy that enables you to bridge to the oceanic realms while on Earth.

This part of you enters through the doors and walks towards you. You connect with the magnificent light of this being until you feel yourself merge with it completely.

You may spend more time with the council, communicating with them if you choose, until you feel your time is complete.

You follow Lady Neptune out of the temple and towards a cylinder of light waiting for you.

You step into the cylinder of light and allow it to transport you to the surface.

At the surface you see that you have been transported near the shore. You thank Lady Neptune. She disappears back into the water and you glide to the shore and to the sanctuary of your home.

Meditation to Awaken One's Toning Ability

Sit quietly in meditation.

Float above your body and allow your spirit to guide you towards the direction of the ocean.

Fly out into the middle of the ocean and visualise diving deep into the water.

Travel through the water until you see the glowing white light of the sea moon and the sea kingdoms.

Follow an illuminated path on the sea floor towards the ancient sound stones in the sea. These are tall standing stones that hum or 'sing'.

See these stones in front of you. Energy travels from these sound stones into your body, into your heart and then out through your voice and into your energy field, and when facilitating a healing, the energy field of the client.

Use the tone to sweep through your energy field, or the client's energy field, and lift out disruptive energies, sending them to Archangel Michael, and/or directly home to the fifth dimension.

Clearing Lower Spirits or Entities in Client's Energy Fields

Occasionally a channel/healer will be called upon to lift a lower spirit or entity out of a client's energy field. In these instances, when one realises one has encountered a lower or even sinister being in a client's energy field, usually through sensing it while attempting the Energy Field Clearing Meditation, it is essential to call upon the power and integrity of Archangel Michael. He will escort this lower or sinister being from the client's energy field in the proper way. A channel/healer must not attempt to coax this being to the light herself or to engage in any telepathic dialogue with the being. The channel must refuse to be drawn into the being's karma or the karma between the being and the client. The being's desire to engage the channel in conversation is an attempt to entangle the channel in the karmic interplay between the being and the client or initialise an entirely new karmic cycle between the being and the channel.

It is strongly recommended never to open one's channels to such a being through sympathy or curiosity. This level of engagement entraps the channel and may cause the lower or sinister being to gain a foothold in the channel's energy field. As soon as a channel suspects or detects a lower spirit, the channel must act swiftly and without hesitation before sympathy or curiosity takes hold, calling upon Archangel Michael immediately to initiate its healing or transmutation. The channel must be wary of believing that she has the power or ability to 'redeem' a lower spirit. Her role is to serve her client and leave the redemption of lower spirits to the higher councils and Archangel Michael.

Providing the channel's energy field is clear, the channel does not have any dominating disruptive lower aspects and that Archangel Michael is called upon to assist, the lower or sinister being will move on quickly, usually within moments. Because one never knows when a lower or sinister being will present in a client's energy field, one must be vigilant in ensuring one's energy field is clear of debris. It is for this reason and for the clarity of one's channelled messages that a practising channel/healer must refrain from behaviours and substances that muddy one's energy field, such as excessive alcohol consumption and mind-altering drugs. One should never facilitate a

healing or channelling after one has consumed alcohol or is under the influence of mind-altering substances.

Clearing as an Ongoing Commitment

As has been emphasised throughout, when preparing to channel to others,
it is important that one clears one's energy field of all debris - unresolved
aspects and external pollution. For a happier life in general, it is tremen-
dously helpful to keep one's home, workplace and energy field clear of debris.
Lavender oil and amethyst crystal help to clear the energy field of energetic
toxins. Place some lavender oil in a spray bottle with water and spray one's
energy field regularly. It is also a good idea to burn certain aromatherapy
oils in the work place or even in the home if the energy in those places feels
heavy. Lavender oil is a natural energetic antiseptic. Sage oil and lemongrass
are both strong energetic cleansers whether used separately or together.
Spearmint oil can clear the etheric residue of chemical toxins and can be
useful to repair the energy field after surgery. Cinnamon aromatherapy oil
offers very strong protection for the energy field and can clear fourth dimensional psychic interference. Frankincense has similar spiritual properties
and can also clear the third eye of interference. One must use one's intuition
and choose the oils that feel appropriate. By burning resins or oils in an
oil burner through the home or office and putting them is a spray bottle
and spraying these oils, one calls upon the essences of herbs and flowers to
cleanse the space of the unseen level of debris that impact on human energy
fields.

Bach Flower Remedies, Bush Flower Essences and similar products as well as
homeopathic treatments can all cleanse the energy field of other clusters of
debris that are not understood by the human eye. These layers of debris can
create confusion in one's mind and in one's energy fields. Just because people
generally cannot see these layers of debris, does not mean they do not have
an effect. Again, engage in the meditation from Part One to clear away any
debris, lower spirits and entities - and continue to do so on a regular basis.

Do the Aspect Therapy Meditation when feeling isolated, agitated or frustrated. All initiates know when their energy field is out of balance because
the world reflects it back to them very quickly. One must train oneself to
observe what enters one's life and what is reflected back to oneself as an

indicator of the state of one's energy field. When an initiate attracts a pattern or a situation that repeats itself, it is important to enter into meditation and look at the aspect that is trying to get attention by creating a situation that repeats itself regularly.

Remember that aspects want to be cleared, they do not want to be separate and they want to come home. If an aspect does not want to come home or is being rebellious and difficult, it is because not all of the elements regarding the aspect have been identified or there may be another aspect underpinning that aspect. It is important to keep clearing aspects until the energy clears completely.

As a general reminder, utilise the meditation from Part One to cleanse away any thoughts that do not serve one's highest good in overall terms. If one has children, ask one's Gateway Guardian for permission from the childrens' higher selves to clear their energy fields. Enter into meditation, visualise each child's energy field and use the technique of shining light in their energy fields to clear away debris. Sometimes children pick up these lower energies from school or sporting clubs. Helping them to keep their energy fields clear of debris will help them to be more confident and happier in themselves. External debris can wear on a person's self-esteem and so one may notice powerful differences in one's children through consciously clearing them of this sort of debris.

Take note of positive changes in one's life and the lives of one's children that unfold as a direct result of following the Gateway Guardian's advice. This evidence of improvement helps to build trust towards this being. If ever this trust weakens, enter into meditation and tell the Gateway Guardian rather than unconsciously pull away or dismiss the spiritual path altogether.

And finally...

Remember to keep updating one's connection to the channelling system. This is not a complicated process. It is simply about asking a question in meditation, allowing some quiet space and having the patience to allow the answer to come. The more this is practised, the stronger and more developed the channelling system becomes. In time, one will be able to allow one's Gateway Guardian to speak through one's own voice freely or will be able to simply put pen to paper and write down the Gateway Guardian's information clearly.

As one works with one's Gateway Guardian, other beings of light may join in to assist with one's training to integrate their frequency or channel into one's own channelling system so that one can communicate with them directly too. A channelling system has the capacity to hold a multitude of channels to many different beings of light and entire realms simultaneously. When a different guide or being of light presents, simply follow the same process of asking that being to stand in Archangel Michael's energy field and receive the Divine light from above. Allow the Divine light to flow through the whole length of that being's body. In this way, one is certain that the being serves one's highest good and will and is aligned to the Law of One and fifth dimensional consciousness.

Once the channelling system is active and 'open of business' it is likely that one will attract other guides and beings who would like to channel through. Sometimes an initiate may have hundreds of channels open at the same time to all sorts of beings such as enlightened masters, angels and saints. For a particular client whom one sees regularly or to whom one is deeply connected, one may have a semi-permanent channel to the client's higher self. In this case, it is also important that one's channelling encourages the client to connect to her own guidance also.

Remember, too, every person has the ability to receive channelled information. It is always helpful as a channel to want to teach others to develop the same connection with themselves and their own Gateway Guardian because ultimately, one should want to become redundant, where one's clients develop the confidence and the security in themselves, to trust their own channels and discover their self sovereignty. As a channel, one must work in a way that allows one to feel comfortable with who one is and one's mission on Earth. It is important to make the commitment to serve the highest good and the highest assignment, supporting others to feel confident about their spiritual journey, and facilitating higher connections for others so that they too can connect to their own higher guidance and receive messages for themselves.

The channel's path in service to the Spiritual Hierarchy for Earth is deeply rewarding and personally enriching. May every channel experience the rewards of a life dedicated to spiritual service, aligned to Divine Will, in the form that Divine Will decides.

Definition of Terms

All That Is

All that is, was and ever will be manifest, suffused with the energy of the Source or Creator who manifests as any and all of creation, so that Creator and Creation are One in reality and in divinity.

Aspects

Internal characters or part of oneself. If the Soul is a small pool of water, the aspects are the drops of water that make up the pool. Each drop of water is as important as the other as each drop comes together to make the whole. Likewise, it is essential to the overall wellbeing of the 'pool' that each drop of water is as clear as possible and aligned to Divine Will. Any pollution or lack of alignment in a single drop of water will pull down the vibration of the whole pool. Hence the importance of Aspect Therapy and other like therapies, as a way of cleansing the individual drops or water or Aspects of Self.

Aspect Therapy

Integration of all our internal characters. Integration of sub-personalities. 'Aspect Therapy' is a technique to cleanse individual aspects to ensure that they work in harmony with the whole.

Blueprint

When the spirit/aspect enters into the womb and into its physical form prior to its birth, it brings with it a divine plan. This divine plan is a blueprint created by the Incarnation Council. Contained in the blueprint is the information the aspect requires throughout its life. This blueprint is like an internal navigation system that leads the human through the various stages and choices that present upon the life path.

Body Cell Memory

All physical experiences are stored in the memory banks of the body. These memory banks or storehouses are located in the cells of the body. The cells store physical memories in their memory banks. The physical experiences of the body are stored to become Body Cell Memory.

Dimensions

Realms of vibrational existence.

Third Dimension

Esoterically understood as the animal kingdom. For the human being, the third dimension provides the opportunity to develop self-consciousness. Creation develops an attachment to life and thus develops the Will to Survive. Such attachment creates awareness of that which may damage or end life and thus fear is born. Humans exist in the third dimension or lower levels of the fourth dimension until they evolve themselves beyond their primary focus on survival and desire to survive, to the more spiritual aspirations of the upper fourth dimension.

Fourth Dimension

The fourth dimension is known as the human kingdom, as the abilities and sensibilities a person aligns to in the fourth dimension reflect the truer nature of a human being than that of the behaviours and beliefs a person adopts as a product of existing in the third dimension. In this dimension, creation seeks to reconnect to and reclaim its connection to its higher self and to the Divine.

Fifth Dimension

The fifth dimension is the spiritual kingdom. By the time the initiate reaches this kingdom, he/she is already well aware of the purpose of his incarnation, and the meaning of his life. This dimension does not carry the duality of love and fear like the fourth dimension does, and is the home base of Love. The Law of One is fully established in the fifth dimension.

Divine Will

Divine Will is the manifested intention of the Divine Father/Mother of the All That Is. There is no presence higher than this.

Divine Will is the complete will of the Divine Presence that underwrites all activity throughout the All That Is that is initiated by those beings aligned to Divine Will. Divine Will is received as the universal principle of harmony that exists in all things within this universe.

Divine Will serves the highest benefit of all beings within the All That Is, observing the universal principle of harmony that organises all things within the All That Is to allow for the perfect synchronicity and symphony of frequencies that encompasses all that is created and yet to be created within the All That Is.

Hierarchy

Spiritual Hierarchy for Earth

The Spiritual Hierarchy for Earth was formed before Earth's creation. It is the governing body of the planet. It consists of twelve founding individual hierarchies. As Earth developed, interest in her grew and thus did the Spiritual Hierarchy for Earth receive new individual members from different parts of the galaxy, however the founding members remain and are the core of the governing body.

One's own hierarchy

Every person on Earth belongs to a hierarchy. A human being is either a member of one of the original twelve hierarchies that established the Spiritual Hierarchy for Earth or from a hierarchy that joined Earth at a later stage in her development. One's hierarchy is constructed of geometric light designs and sound, which houses and organises the many parts of one's soul that one's soul has chosen to send to Earth and other planetary worlds and realms for experience. One's hierarchy, while participating in the grand assignment to restore Earth to the light, is connected to the Spiritual Hierarchy for Earth and the planet Earth herself.

Central Sun Hierarchy

The name given to one of the twelve hierarchies that make up the founding members of the Spiritual Hierarchy for Earth (one of the few whose name is well established).

Higher Self

The higher self is the station into which other aspects of one's hierarchy connect and then reach down into one's physical body on Earth. The higher self is the director of the plan for one's physicality and time upon Earth and administers the practical components of the Earth assignment.

Higher Self and Incarnation Team Level

The Higher Self and Incarnation Team level is an etheric office that sits well above a human incarnate's crown chakra and serves him during his physical life on Earth. The access point to this level is in the fourth dimension. The initiate gains access to all other levels of his hierarchy through the Higher Self and Incarnation Team level as well as the heightened awareness and spiritual gifts of the fourth dimension. For this reason, this level is considered the gateway to full spiritual awareness of one's hierarchy and multidimensional existence.

The Higher Self and Incarnation Team takes care to meet the physical needs of the human incarnate according to what he has chosen for his earthly experience. This level reads how he is and then relays the information back to the other relevant councils. The Higher Self monitors how the human incarnate is coping with the Earth assignment, how the physical body is responding to different stresses and experiences, and whether it needs extra or specific assistance. The Higher Self and Incarnation Team works out which channels are integrating in the channelling system, which ones are not, and looks after the technical side of the spiritual channelling system of the human body. This level also listens to the human incarnate's requests, questions, suggestions and complaints and endeavours to find solutions where appropriate.

Human Initiate (referred to in the text as an 'initiate')

A spiritual being who has incarnated in human form with the intention to complete a spiritual assignment, spiritually awaken, or ascend on Earth while maintaining a human body.

Your Hierarchy

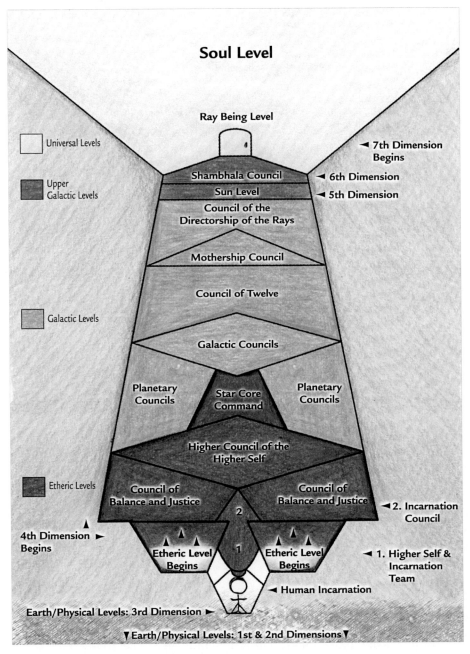

Soul Level

Ray Being Level

Universal Levels

Upper Galactic Levels

Shambhala Council — 6th Dimension
Sun Level — 5th Dimension

7th Dimension Begins

Council of the Directorship of the Rays

Mothership Council

Council of Twelve

Galactic Levels

Galactic Councils

Planetary Councils   Star Core Command   Planetary Councils

Higher Council of the Higher Self

Etheric Levels

Council of Balance and Justice   Council of Balance and Justice

2. Incarnation Council

2

4th Dimension Begins

Etheric Level Begins   1   Etheric Level Begins

1. Higher Self & Incarnation Team

Human Incarnation

Earth/Physical Levels: 3rd Dimension

Earth/Physical Levels: 1st & 2nd Dimensions

Keys

Information banks of higher technology, colour, sound, light and memory. These information banks are encoded into a person's body or places in the Earth. These are released in a person's body or area on Earth when the individual or area is moving into a new vibration or higher frequency. The releasing of keys in certain parts of the Earth or in one's human body at a pre-ordained time may also activate one's awakening or ascension. Human beings can carry keys for each other and the higher realms can utilise awakened human beings to transfer keys to other human beings who may or may not have awakened.

Law of One

The Law of One states that: *When all are allowed to be within their frequencies, all shall come into peace and into harmony.*

Over-lighting Devas

The Over-lighter's, or the 'Over-lighting devas', are an integral part of the nature kingdom. This group of beings are the over-lighting and overseeing spirits of plants, trees, lakes, rivers and the earth itself.

Signature Frequency

The signature frequency is the indestructible essence of a soul - the soul's quintessence that cannot be tainted or altered or removed from the Oneness. Full knowledge of the signature frequencies exists on a scale and is of an intricacy that cannot be perceived by humankind. It is the Great Mystery, the essence of which remains forever in the hands of the Most Ancient Heavenly and Divine Father and is to be coveted by none. He who is known in this realm of Earth as Archangel Michael remains, as he has for eons, the protector and guard of the Great Mystery of the Signature Frequencies.

Spiritual Family

The Spiritual Family is a grand structure consisting of the twelve hierarchies, which are the ancient families of this universe. The Office of the Central Sun sits in the core of the structure, and although it is technically part of the Central Sun Hierarchy, its frequencies and facility is available to all. The Spiritual Family has different names depending on the level and frequencies it is operating on. An umbrella name frequently used to unify the family is Arkamusha. The High Council of Arkamusha serves the twelve hierarchies that make up the Spiritual Family and is made up of the highest levels of the Divine Mother and Divine Father of each hierarchy. The home base of the High Council of Arkamusha is the seventh dimension, although its members travel frequently between the dimensions according to their assignments.

Spiritual Hierarchy for Earth

See 'Hierarchy'.

Other books by Amanda Guggenheimer

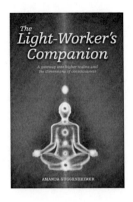

The Light-Worker's Companion

The Light-Worker's Companion supports readers who are awakening to, or are already consciously on, their spiritual pathway.

The Companion seeks to be exactly so, a companion and a friend to those who desire a deeper connection with themselves and the Beings of Light guiding them.

The Light-Worker's Companion focuses on topics that facilitate a higher connection such as dimensions of consciousness, spiritual assignments, Ascension, and the spiritual family who offer their assistance in the process.

The work is a guidebook to the many levels of Ascension and awareness one might experience as an initiate on the spiritual path. It empowers the spiritual seeker by providing channelled information, and then invites the reader to assimilate that knowledge by following the meditations that accompany those messages. The combination of channelled information and practical exercises strengthens in the reader, a sense of deep spiritual connection.

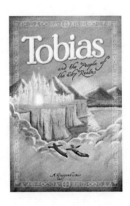

Tobias and the People of the Sky Realms

Tobias and the People of the Sky Realms is a fiction for the spiritually awakening teenager, and also of interest to the adult light-worker seeking to understand the higher realms through the medium of a story rather than a non-fiction work.

"When an ethereal stranger climbed through Tobias's bedroom window in the middle of the night, the young man had no idea that she came to claim him for a vital mission. Her world, in the Sky Realms above earth, suffered from a dark enemy. That enemy lived on earth and also worked to enslave human minds.

After visiting the Sky Realms, Tobias realises he has little choice but to help his new friend and her family. The future of the Sky Realms and earth depended upon it. In battle, he prays for the courage to do what is expected of him, not realising that a long-lost part of himself, caught in another time, could undermine the entire mission."

For more information please visit
www.amandaguggenheimer.com